MEDITATION AND MENTAL HEALTH

MEDITATION

AND

MENTAL HEALTH

an introduction to

AWARENESS BASED COGNITIVE THERAPY

Peter Wilberg

2010

New Yoga Publications

First published by New Yoga Publications, Whitstable
www.thenewyoga.org

Printed and bound in the United States of America by CreateSpace.com

ISBN 978-1-904519-14-0

Note to the Reader

This book, like all other New Yoga Publications, not only adds to but also draws from Peter Wilberg's entire body of writings on 'The Awareness Principle' and its Practice – what he terms 'The New Yoga of Awareness'. Consequently the reader is asked to bear in mind that some repetitions of textual content, both across and within particular works, has been unavoidable. It is hoped that this will not be an annoyance or hindrance to the reader, but rather serve to refresh and reinforce the reader's understanding – as well as ensuring that each new publication contains material drawn from Peter Wilberg's most recent and refined conceptual articulations of the key 'Principles and Practices of Awareness' he presents. For these continue to evolve in line with his on-going research, meditative practice and therapeutic application of those Principles.

CONTENTS

Introduction

What is the relation between meditation and mental health? What does it mean to 'meditate'? Instead of medicating 'mental illness' can we use meditation to *actively affirm and find meaning* in all that we experience – even states of mental, emotional or somatic 'ill-health' – whilst at the same time freeing ourselves from entrapment by them?

This selection of essays offers a new understanding of 'meditation' as a set of basic principles and practices of awareness which allow us to do just that – to both affirm our conscious experience in all its dimensions, 'positive' or 'negative', whilst at the same time freeing ourselves from identification with them.

These practices have a powerful therapeutic value – not just in relation to 'mental' health but also somatic illness. They include:

1. taking 'intervals' or 'breathing spaces' of time between all focussed daily activities to just *be aware* of our body, self and life-world as a whole.

2. reminding ourselves that the pure awareness of any experienced thought or emotion is *not itself* a thought or emotion – but innately free of thoughts and emotions.

3. 'coming to our senses' – giving awareness to our immediate sensual experience of mental or emotional states, attending to where and how we feel them in our bodies.

4. patiently awaiting the 'out of the blue' insights that invariably arise *from awareness* if we give ourselves all the time we need to 'meditate' – to be aware of – our felt, bodily sense of distress or 'dis-ease'.

Such practices are not simply an eclectic toolkit of psychological theories, techniques and meditational aids.

Instead they are all integrated by a single unifying philosophical principle – 'The Awareness Principle'.

This is a refinement of Indian 'Advaita' or 'Non-Dual' philosophy, and as such completely transcends conventional Western concepts of 'cognition', 'consciousness' and 'mind'. From it follow the many Practices of Awareness that together constitute what I call 'The New Yoga of Awareness'.

'Awareness Based Cognitive Therapy' (ABCT) is the 'ABC' of this 'New Yoga' – being *a selection* of its basic practices designed specifically to offer new and effective approaches to both mental and physical ill-health.

As well as transforming our everyday lives and relationships these practices can be incorporated in the work of counsellors, therapists, health, educational and social-work professionals of all sorts.

Their aim however, is not merely to repair the effects of living in a mad world of manic 'busy-ness' – one whose pace and pressures is almost designed to deprive us of time and space for meditative *awareness* – and us thus is in itself a *constantly renewed source* of anxiety, stress, depression and other mental health problems. Instead the purpose of ABCT is to offer people – including both patients and health professionals – the means by which to inwardly guard a time and space for meditative awareness – to create 'breathing spaces of awareness' despite and in the face of all social and economic time pressures and demands.

Both 'physical' and 'mental' health do indeed have a social and relational as well as an individual dimension. Neither however, are essentially to do with 'mind' in the Western sense (a sense unfortunately carried by the term 'mindfulness'). Instead the foundation of both health and sanity is a *mind- and thought-free awareness* that allows to 'come to our senses' in the most literal sense – revivifying our immediate *bodily and sensory experiencing* of ourselves, other people and the world around us.

'Thoughts' themselves are not merely more or less accurate 'reflections' or 'representations' of our subjectively experienced reality or life-world – they are themselves elements *of* that reality – *experienced* as 'cognitive events' in the form of mental words or speech. Thus what the major theorists of Cognitive Therapies refer to as 'meta-cognitive awareness' is an awareness of *thoughts themselves* as *subjective experiences* rather than 'objective' cognitions.

Within the framework of Awareness Based Cognitive Therapy on the other hand, 'meta-cognitive' awareness is understood as the very *essence* of *awareness as such* – and recognised as the most primordial mode of cognition *per se*. That is because awareness is the *precondition* for our experience of any thought or thing, self, world of universe whatsoever.

What is termed 'mindfulness' or 'meta-cognitive awareness' – is in essence, nothing more or less than *awareness as such*. As such it is no mere theoretical catchword or practical panacea for those driven to despair or madness by a mad world. For awareness is not only – in principle – *the* most primordial mode of cognition *per se* – transcending both mental and perceptual cognition. It is also and above all the restoration of *dignity* to all of us in our search to find a sane and healthy way of 'being-in-time' and 'being-in-the-world' – through *taking time to be aware* – and through learning to rest in and *be* that very *awareness*.

Part 1 of the book introduces this philosophy of awareness as a paradigmatic life principle and practice.

Part 2 introduces in theory and practice a new awareness-based understanding of the nature of 'meditation'.

Part 3 contrast The Awareness Principle and its roots in Indian Advaitic ('Non-Dual') philosophy with the dominant paradigms of Western psychology and counselling practice, introducing the new paradigm of 'Non-Dual Therapy' – of which Awareness Based Cognitive Therapy is a refined expression. It ends with a selection of 'Aphorisms on Awareness' showing their sources in Indian thought.

Part 4 present a complete introduction to 'Awareness Based Cognitive Therapy' as such, contrasting it with both traditional CBT methodology and MBCT, as well as showing, through a brief case report[*], how the 'Primary Principles and Practices' of ABCT can be effectively applied.

Part 5 explores the specific relevance of the awareness paradigm to 'depression' as well as exploring its relation to complex psychoanalytic concepts such as Kleinian 'object relations' theory and Lacanian analysis, and modern 'mentalisation' based therapies.

Part 6 goes on to present an awareness-based approach to 'physical' as well as 'mental' illness – thus challenging, in principle, both their separation and the entire medical model of illness *per se*.

The 1st appendix to the book emphasises even further the importance of 'meditation' as opposed to 'medication' in approaching mental health problems – offering a significant 'health warning' to therapists and counsellors regarding the often unseen or mis-read symptoms stemming from the use of or addiction to prescription drugs such as anti-depressants.

The 2nd appendix summarises once again the key philosophical precepts of 'The Awareness Principle' as a new foundation for life and science, medicine and psychology.

The 3rd appendix offers a brief introduction to the methodology of 'Personalised Training in ABCT', along with contact details for those interest in pursuing such training, whether independently, or as a form of Continued Professional Development allowing them to incorporate the basic principles and practices of ABCT into their current professional work.

---

[*] contributed by Karin Heinitz, UKCP registered Psychotherapist

Part 1

The Primary Distinction and
The Primary Choice

If people get lost in thoughts, emotions or everyday activities, then they may be 'conscious' but they are not necessarily 'aware'. Drawing on specific traditions of Indian thought, Awareness Based Cognitive Therapy (ABCT) re-introduces a fundamental or 'primary' philosophical distinction – between 'consciousness' and 'awareness'.

'Consciousness' is awareness *of* something – of some *focus* of awareness or element of our experience, whether a mood, emotion, impulse or thought. 'Awareness' on the other hand, is understood as consciousness *as such* – distinct, like empty space, from all its contents.

If consciousness is characterised by a type of *focal awareness*, then awareness is a 'defocused' consciousness or *field consciousness*. By learning to distinguish awareness in this sense from all experienced *contents* of consciousness – whether mental, emotional, perceptual or somatic – we are freed from unaware *identification* with these contents.

Think of all you are experiencing at any point in time – whether inwardly or outwardly, physically or emotionally – together with all your mental reflections on your experience – as one side of a coin or line. Think of the other side of the coin or line as nothing but the very awareness of experiencing it. The two sides of that coin or line are inseparable – and yet they are also absolutely distinct.

The Awareness Principle is based on this *primary distinction* – drawing a line between anything we *experience* and the pure *awareness* of experiencing it.

things we experience

---

the awareness of experiencing those things

This 'Primary Distinction' – between all that we consciously experience and the pure *awareness* of experiencing it – is part of the unitary life principle that I term 'The Awareness Principle'. From it follow the many simple but powerful 'Practices of Awareness' that make up what I call 'The New Yoga of Awareness'.

One primary Practice of Awareness following from 'The Primary Distinction' is what I term 'The Primary Choice'. This is the choice to identify with the pure *awareness* of whatever we are experiencing rather than identifying with one or more elements of that experiencing. By 'elements of experiencing' I mean anything from an outwardly experienced object, situation, event or action, to an inwardly experienced impulse, sensation, mood, emotion, memory, anticipation or thought.

In writings on Eastern spiritual teachings too much mystery is usually made of the idea of a 'pure' or 'transcendental' awareness that is free of thoughts, emotions, drives and desires etc. and the 'effort' needed to attain this awareness. In reality, if The Awareness Principle is understood, no great effort at all is required to attain this state of pure or 'transcendental' awareness. The awareness of a physical object such as a leather chair is not itself a chair and nor is that awareness made of leather. Neither is the *awareness* of a thought itself a thought. Similarly, the awareness of any 'thing' (whether an object, situation, event, mood, emotion, desire, impulse, action, thought etc.) is *not itself* a 'thing' or 'thought' of any sort. The 'awareness principle' is simply the recognition that *awareness – in principle* – is innately 'pure', both thought-free and 'thing-free' in general. It does not need to be effortfully 'emptied' of any thoughts or things to be *made* 'pure'. For just as space is absolutely distinct from all the objects within it, so also is awareness as such absolutely distinct from all its contents – from all we are aware *of*. It does not need to be 'emptied' of all content to be as clear and pure as the 'empty' space around objects.

Introduction to the Practice of Awareness:

1. Eyes open. simply allow yourself time to be aware of all the different things you are currently experiencing within and without – from physical objects around you to inner emotions and thoughts. Then become more aware of the clear space around your body, and around all the physical objects in your environment. Feel a similar clear space around any 'things' you are experiencing within you, such as emotions and thoughts. In this way you will come to *experience* the clear *space-like* quality of *awareness as such* rather than just experiencing particular things *within* this space of awareness.

All the Practices of Awareness that make up 'The New Yoga of Awareness' are based on passing from a new awareness of all that we experience to a new experience of *awareness as such* – in this case *as* the clarity and translucency of empty space, or alternatively as light, or as vitalising air and breath (the meaning of the term *prana.*

2. Sitting comfortably with your eyes open, take two to ten minutes to simply be aware of what you are currently experiencing within you. Note down on paper or make a mental note of the different elements of your experiencing, distinguishing them into three categories as below.

PHYSICAL SENSATIONS	EMOTIONAL FEELINGS	THOUGHTS AND QUESTIONS
example: a fluttering sensation in the stomach	example: feeling 'anxious'	example: how can I best say something to person X?

Emotional terms such as 'anxious', 'upset', 'depressed' etc. are actually just umbrella labels for a huge variety of possible physical states and feelings. Concentrate on your direct bodily experience of emotional states and not on the emotional labels for them. If your accompanying thoughts take the form 'I am anxious' or 'I am depressed', ask yourself what exactly it is you are anxious, angry or depressed about, yet without looking for a 'cause' to blame them on, whether an event or situation, thing or person. Recognise instead that any disturbing feeling is essentially a *felt question* – a question felt but not yet clearly formulated. Yet by simply *feeling* your feelings in a sensuous bodily way, new ways of formulating their meaning or 'sense' – the *question* you are feeling through them – will arise in your mind. Then there will be no need to label your emotions – or see the sole question as how to 'deal' with those feelings.

The twin precepts of 'The Awareness Principle' are that (a) awareness is everything, and (b) everything in turn *is* an awareness. 'Awareness Based Cognitive Therapy' rooted in the recognition that everything we are aware *of* is at the same time an awareness or 'cognition' in its own right. A question is also an *awareness*. Giving *more* awareness to things thus allows us to recognise the particular awareness or cognition that it essentially *is*. An 'inner' feeling for example, is not just something we happen to be aware *of* within us, but is itself a *wordless cognitive awareness* of something in our 'outer' world. Hence the importance of *feeling* feelings with our *bodies* rather than automatically labelling them in words and objectifying them in our minds. For feelings can, paradoxically, only transform into more aware 'mental' questions and cognitions by patiently 'meditating' or 'ruminating' them – giving them more wordless *bodily* awareness.

We are as much aware of our *self* as a whole as we are aware of our *bodies* and of our *life-world* as a whole. Such simple practices of awareness as those introduced above ultimately allow us to identify with that Self which does not simply 'have' or 'possess' awareness but *is* awareness. This is not an awareness that is 'yours' or 'mine' – the private property of an ego or 'I'. Instead it is that awareness and that Self [the *Atman*] which Indian thought understood as the *source* of all individualised selves or 'consciousnesses', having the character of a universal space or 'field' of awareness from and within which all things arise – and of which all things are but shapes or expressions.

From Focal to Field Awareness

The Awareness Principle and the Practice of Awareness are about how the power of awareness can transform our consciousness and free our everyday lives from all that is a source of dis-ease for us.

Again, if people get lost in watching TV or playing computer games, in work or domestic chores, in thinking or talking, in worrying about life or in feeling particular emotions, pains – or even pleasures – then they may be 'conscious' but they are not aware.

Whenever our consciousness becomes overly focussed or fixated on any one thing we are conscious of, dominated by it or identified with it, we lose awareness.

For unlike ordinary 'consciousness', awareness is not focussed on any one thing we experience. Awareness is more like the space surrounding us and surrounding all things we are aware of. For space is not the same as any 'thing' within it.

Living with and within awareness is like truly living with and within space – which both encompasses but is also absolutely distinct from each and every thing within it.

To transform our ordinary consciousness into awareness therefore, means first of all becoming more aware of space itself – both the outer space around us and surrounding things, and also the inner space surrounding our thoughts, feelings, impulses and sensations.

Enhancing our bodily awareness of the space around us is the first step to helping us to experience space itself – outer and inner – as an expansive spacious field of awareness – a field free of domination by anything we may be conscious of or experience within it.

'Achieving freedom through awareness' therefore means transforming our ordinary consciousness or 'focal awareness' into a new type of spacious 'field awareness' – for this is the true and literal meaning of 'expanding' our consciousness.

If we are able to sense and identify with the spacious awareness field around and within us, then we can do two things. We can both freely acknowledge and affirm everything we experience or are conscious of within that field – whether pleasant or unpleasant. And yet at the same time we can stop our 'consciousness' getting sucked into, stuck on, focussed or fixated on any one thing.

The capacity to constantly come back to the spacious awareness field frees us from all the things our consciousness normally gets so fixated on that we can no longer distinguish or free ourselves from them. True freedom is freedom from identification with anything we experience – anything we are 'conscious' or 'aware' OF. This freedom comes from sensing and identifying with that spacious awareness field within which we experience all things, outwardly and inwardly.

Awareness is not the same as what is often called 'mindfulness' – for it includes awareness of all we experience as mind or mental activity.

An old spiritual tradition has it that awareness itself is 'God' – understood as an infinitely spacious field of consciousness. This tradition also understood awareness as the source of all beings and as the eternal core or essence of our being – as our higher self. Just as through enhanced awareness of space we can experience it as a boundlessly expansive awareness field, so can we also experience our own spiritual core or essence as a powerful centre of awareness within that field.

Most forms of therapy or counselling are limited by the fact that they do not distinguish 'consciousness' or 'focal awareness' from field awareness. They themselves focus the client's consciousness on its contents – on things they are conscious or unconscious of – rather than transforming that focal consciousness into a clear and spacious awareness field – and centring the client's awareness in that field.

Both the Awareness Principle and the Practice of Awareness are founded on a primary distinction between consciousness and awareness, between any thing we are consciously experiencing on the one hand, and the pure awareness of experiencing it on the other. Identifying this pure awareness with space is the most effective way of experiencing it.

This primary distinction offers us in turn a primary choice – either to identify ourselves with things we are conscious of, or to identify instead with the very awareness of them – an awareness that will automatically free our consciousness from domination by any of its contents, anything we experience.

An important help in making this choice is to remind yourself of a simple truth: that just as awareness of an object is not itself an object, so is awareness of a thought, emotion or physical sensation not itself a thought, emotion or sensation. Awareness of any thoughts you have is something innately thought-free – just as awareness of any impulses, emotions and sensations you feel is something innately free of those impulses, emotions or sensations. Awareness is Freedom.

Living without - and with - Awareness

LIVING WITHOUT AWARENESS	LIVING WITH AWARENESS

A man wakes up in the morning. He feels grumpy and annoyed. The first thing that comes into his mind are feelings left over from what his partner has said on the previous evening, words that annoyed and left him feeling hurt.

He turns the conversation over and over in his head while he prepares to go to work. The more he thinks about it the angrier he gets, feeling not only justifiably 'hurt' but hateful in a way he dare not express.

He wants to find a way of putting his feelings of hurt and anger out of his mind and stop thinking about them, yet at the same time feels an impulse to let them out on his partner in an explosive and hateful way.

Caught in this dilemma, he thinks, how can he possibly concentrate on work feeling all this?

Identifying with this thought he does indeed end up

A man wakes up in the morning. He feels grumpy and annoyed. The first thing that comes into his mind is the row he had with his partner on the previous evening, the words that annoyed him and left him feeling hurt.

This time he is more aware however. Instead of just letting his mind run on, so fixated on his feelings and identified with them that they get stronger in a way he 'knows' will ruin his day – he practices awareness.

First he says to himself 'It is not that I AM grumpy, annoyed or hurt'. "I am simply AWARE of feelings of 'grumpiness', 'annoyance' and 'hurt'. I AM AWARE also, that the more I focus on them the stronger these feelings become, and I am aware too of the THOUGHT – not the 'fact' – that this will 'ruin my day."

Then he takes a second major step. Instead of identifying with these feelings being unconcentrated, closed off and distracted all day, with no resolution of his feelings in sight.

When he comes home and sees his partner again he is still torn between repressing his feelings and expressing them in a vengeful way.

He feels even angrier towards her as a result of feeling himself in this conflicted state, seeing it too, as her fault. As a result, his feelings spiral even more in intensity and at the same time he tries to reign them inside his body, contracting the space he feels inside his body and making him feel even more explosive.

She in turn picks up his reigned-in emotions and bodily tenseness and finally unable to bear or contain the tensions herself says something that bursts the bubble, letting him explode in anger.

The result is that she now feels angry and hurt, and (another) mighty row results.

The row itself does not resolve anything or lead to new and helpful insights that and this thought he chooses to identify with the simple AWARENESS of them.

He does so first by reminding himself that the AWARENESS of any thought or emotion is not itself a thought or emotion. Instead it is more like a free and empty space in which all thoughts and feelings can be held and affirmed − yet without becoming filled, dominated and preoccupied by them. He succeeds in identifying with AWARENESS by becoming deliberately more aware of the actual space around his body, sensing it as a larger, unfilled space around and between his thoughts and feelings too.

As a result of putting himself in this more expansive space, he no longer feels a need to close off, tense and tighten his body in order to prevent himself exploding with the feelings and thoughts that filled it. For he knows that this tightening is exactly what contracts his inner space and makes it feel so full.

He no longer feels himself 'in a space' that is so

raise their awareness of important aspects of themselves and their relationship.

Instead it just leaves them temporarily relieved or emptied of their feelings – whilst at the same time still harbouring the same thoughts and judgements towards one another, regarding each other as the 'cause' of their own thoughts and feelings, and identifying with these feelings and thoughts towards one another.

The next day ends up being no better for either, with both feeling isolated in themselves.

Not able to identify with and feel themselves in a space of awareness big enough to make room for their own feelings – let alone those of their partner – they remain preoccupied with themselves and able to 'contain' their feelings only by contracting and withdrawing into their own separate and isolating spaces.

contracted, crammed and preoccupied by his initial thoughts and feelings, that it leaves no free space of awareness for other important things like his work, and no space too for new insights to arise into the feelings that might have been behind his partner's 'hurtful' words. Such insights do indeed come to him spontaneously in the intervals of his work, and at the end of an undistracted working day.

Still identifying with his sense of being in a space 'big' enough to contain both his own feelings and those of his partner, he is able to not only calmly communicate his feelings but also share his empathic understanding of the feelings that might have been behind the words that 'hurt' him. The result is a hostility-free dialogue which makes them both feel better and more 'together' – feeling once again that they dwell in a shared space of togetherness.

Taking Time to Be Aware

"In robbing us of time, today's culture also robs us of dignity. But dignity has no great value in a culture devoted to progress, power and productivity. Since time is money in modern culture, few of us can afford dignity."

Alexander Lowen

Today's world faces a grave economic, ecological, cultural crisis – indeed a global civilisational crisis. The word 'crisis' means a 'turning point' in time. Humanity has reached a turning point in time, a turning point which requires us to establish a whole new relation to time, a whole new way of being in time, a whole new awareness of time. The nature of that turning point in time, of that new relation to time, that new way of being in time, is simple but profound. Quite simply: it is *taking time to be aware*. Only in this way can human beings find a way of *being-in-time* that is not simply dominated by 'busy-ness' – by *doing* – and aimed only at *having*. The new relation to time that human beings so desperately need at this time of crisis then, is one in which they give themselves time, not just to produce or consume, work or play, but to *be aware*. For to truly 'be' *is* to *be aware*. Just as to truly 'meditate' is simply to *take time to be aware*.

Without granting ourselves time to be aware we impoverish ourselves. For to be aware means to be aware of *all there is* to be aware of – all there is to sense and feel, experience and explore, enjoy and delight in, process and ponder, recollect and anticipate, delve into and draw insight from in the present moment.

Without granting ourselves time to be aware of all that there is to be aware of in the moment, we become overburdened, fatigued, stressed out, depressed or *dis-eased* by all that we have been too rushed to give ourselves time to be aware of. We reduce awareness itself to the next thing to do or say, act on or react to. We reduce being to *doing*. In doing so, we reduce our lives to a series of actions strung out along a two-dimensional timeline. We reduce the moment to a mere point on a timeline, and time itself to a *seemingly* empty space between one moment point and another – one which we have become addicted to filling with *doing*, whether in the form of speaking or acting, working or engaging in 'leisure activities'. Even 'meditation' becomes something to be *done* – for example through the form of the type of bodily stretching engaged in under the name of 'yoga' that substitutes for a meditative stretching and increased mobility of *awareness*.

Doing dominates over *being aware* because all the business powers of this world conspire to keep us *busy* at all costs, not least by forcing us to *sell our time* to employers whose only interest is in exploiting it to the greatest extent possible and making it ever more 'productive'. The old Protestant work ethic with its famous adage – "the Devil makes work for idle hands" – is so instilled in us that *idleness* itself has to be induced by falling sick or aided by the use of drugs, and any idle time we have has to be used to *do* something – if only to take drugs or indulge in activities which either require no awareness or in which we lose all awareness. In this way 'the Devil' does indeed *make* work for idle hands, ensuring even if they are not working they are still *doing*, still not allowing themselves time to just be – to *be aware*.

Yet only by taking *time* to be aware can each of us open up a broader *space* of awareness – one which, like the clear and empty space surrounding things, allows us to meditate, place in perspective and come to new insights regarding whatever questions, concerns or feelings are currently addressing us. Only out of such a *broader*, more spacious and expansive awareness *field* can human beings also come to *deeper*, more thoughtful decisions and find better practical solutions to both personal and world problems. And only out of this broadened and deepened awareness can we also relate to other human beings in a more meditative and aware way – thus bringing about a *healing transformation in human relations*.

All *time-wasting* indecision, mismanagement, misgovernment and mistreatment of others stem from the self-defeating rush of busy-ness that characterises our global business culture. This is a culture of enforced economic conscription of *all* ('employment') which ends up rendering the unique awareness, potentials and creativity of *each* more or less wholly *unemployed*. The value our global capitalist culture places on activity, speed and busy-ness denies the time needed for meditative and aware decision-making – but in this way also slows down or entirely blocks *truly aware, thoughtful and effective action*. Behind this culture is a deep-seated *fear* of awareness, not least awareness of all the ways in which – *lacking awareness* – human beings are destroying each other and the earth.

The resulting global crisis and turning point in time that we now face tells us that it is high time for humanity to become more aware, high time for a cultural revolution in awareness – one based not just on 'slowing down' but on cultivating a whole new way of aware experiencing and action, living and relating, thinking and feeling. This in turn requires new forms of *education in awareness* in all areas of life and knowledge – and not just education in facts or skills. Above all it requires a new understanding of awareness as something essentially distinct from mere consciousness 'of' things. There is all that we experience, all that occurs or goes on in ourselves and the world. And there is *the awareness* of all that occurs or goes on – *the awareness* of all we experience. That awareness – awareness 'as such' or 'pure awareness' – is what alone can free human beings from bondage to anything they are conscious or aware *of*.

Awareness *as such* is a not a product of the brain, bounded by our bodies, or the mere private property of individuals or groups. Instead it has an essentially unbounded and universal character. It is the 'trans-personal' dimension of consciousness. As such, it transcends *identity* – as it also transcends all group *identifications* – social and economic, ethnic, cultural and religious. For awareness itself is the essence of the divine – one and indivisible. That is why anyone who cultivates awareness works not only for their own well-being but for that of the world – a world whose ills all result from a lack of awareness, and thus can never be healed through the politics or psychology of *identity*.

Identification with limiting ways of experiencing ourselves, other people and the world is embedded in our very use of language. Thus instead of *being aware* of having a certain feeling such as anger or sadness, we say "I *am* angry" or "I *am* sad". Instead of being aware of *having* a particular thought or feeling about some thing or person – for example the thought that 'John is a bastard' – we so *identify* with the feelings expressed in that thought that we take it as a 'fact' that 'John *is* a bastard'. As a result of this identification with a limited way of experiencing something or someone, our thoughts and feelings cease to be a true and authentic expression of all there is to be aware of in relation to that thing or person – and make it impossible for us to experience them in different ways. Identified with the 'text' of our thoughts and feelings, we close our awareness to the whole experiential *context* in which they arise. Restricting awareness of the larger context of our experiencing – not being aware of how much *more* there is to be experienced in and through any thing or person – we also restrict the lived 'text' of our own lives and relationships. If the contextual *space* of our awareness is not fully occupied by that text – if we are not wholly *preoccupied* with it – we feel empty and need to fill it with action or emotional drama (whether in ourselves or through television, film and vicarious soap operas).

Herein lies the vicious circle in which individuals and relationships become bound up. For all those things for which we have given ourselves no time-space to become aware of in the *moment* cumulatively mount up in *time* – causing us stress, fatigue or dis-ease, bringing us to a point where we must put a damper on or repress them, or impelling us to impulsively act on them or 'act them out' in an unaware and emotionally reactive and dramatic way. Not living *meditatively* – not granting ourselves time even to be fully aware of how we experience ourselves, we end up with a world in which neither real life people nor fictional characters *have any time for one another*. Instead their lives are reduced to a series of emotional dramas – interspersed by and compensating for periods of uneventful or impoverished experiencing. They have no time for themselves or each other because they give themselves no time to *be aware*. Time itself is measured out purely in *quantities*, and so-called 'quality time' is seen as something to be 'created' only at certain times, rather than as our *birthright* as beings – as a boundless time-space of awareness that can be opened up at any time, within each and every moment of our lives.

'Being aware' means not just attending to the awareness of our thoughts, but also to all the immediate bodily dimensions of our experiencing – to our felt bodily sense of all that is present or going on within and around us. It also means attending to the spaces, inner and outer, within which we experience both ourselves and others, both thoughts and things. In this way we can come to the experience of space itself, inner and outer, as something singular – as a singular, all-embracing time-space of awareness itself.

"Space and time…themselves arise from time-space, which is more primordial than they themselves…"

"Modern man must first and above all find his way back into the full breadth of the space proper to his essence."

Martin Heidegger

Being aware also means learning to feel that we dwell within awareness in the same way that we abide and dwell in the boundlessness of space. Whenever we stop *sensing space*, both within and around us, we contract the space of awareness in which we dwell. Whenever we lose our awareness in thoughts, feelings and everyday activities, rather than attending to *the awareness* of all that we experience around and within us, and whenever we allow our attention to just flit from one thought or action, one *focus of awareness* to another, we lose sense of that larger and more spacious time-space of awareness in which alone we can truly dwell or 'be'.

"You cannot heal a single human being, even with psychotherapy, if you do not first restore his relationship to Being."

Martin Heidegger

It is only out of a primordial *awareness* of being that we first know ourselves and other beings to be in the first place, and thus restore our relationship to Being as such. All theories and sciences, including those of psychology, which simply take their particular objects of enquiry as 'given' – as beings or entities that are simply there as actualities – independently of a prior awareness of them, constitute a denial of this primordial truth, the primordial reality of awareness as such.

Part 2

Meditation as a Practice of Awareness

Many people think, for one reason or another, that they should 'do' something that they call 'meditation'. What they have in mind is maybe going to a meditation class of some sort or 'doing' some form of purely physical 'yoga'. Whether or not they do so however, 'meditation', understood in this way, is taken as just another thing to 'do' – and therefore also just another thing to make time for in their busy or stressful lives. This is a paradox, for the true meaning of meditation does not lie in adding to the list of things we need to make time to do. Indeed, the true meaning of meditation does not lie in making time to 'do' anything at all, nor even making time just to 'be' in some ambiguous way. Instead the meaning of meditation lies in making time *to be aware*. Not at some future time but here and now, and in every moment of our lives.

There is what is 'going on' right now … whatever it is you are doing, thinking, feeling, saying etc. And there is *the awareness* of what is going on – the awareness of whatever it is you are doing, thinking, feeling, saying etc. This awareness embraces not just what is happening in the here and now but its larger *where* and larger *when* – the overall situation and larger life context *within* which it is going on, goes on, and out of which it is emerging. Ultimately it is an awareness that embraces all of space and time.

We say that some people are more sensitive or 'aware' than others. What we mean is that they are generally aware of *more* than others are – more aspects of what is going on, whether in themselves or in others, in the world at large or in the here and now. Those with lesser awareness may have a need to *express* themselves more – for example through therapy – merely to discover just how much more there is for them to be aware of. Those with greater awareness however, may have a no lesser need to express themselves – needing to share all that they may be aware of with others in order not to feel overwhelmed or isolated by that awareness. Both communication and creativity themselves are seen as ways of *giving out* through self-expression, rather than as occasions for fully taking others in, whether through the word or in receptive silence.

As a result, people's social interaction consists simply of talk and telling stories – everyone sharing in words, each for themselves, what is most important to them, whilst their private life is either mute, uncreative and expressionless or else an ongoing search for some form of highly personal self-expression. The fact is however, that we do not need to share all of which we are aware, for awareness itself communicates and transmits itself silently, wordlessly, needing no form of outward expression.

Whether their awareness is greater or lesser, most people have a tendency to identify it with whatever it is they are aware *of*. Not understanding the true nature of awareness they take it as their *own* – as the private property of their ego or 'I'. This is reflected in common ways of speaking. If for example, we are aware of a thought or feeling what we think to ourselves or say to others is '*I* think this' or '*I* feel that'. In doing so we identify ('I-dentify') with whatever it is we are aware *of*. Meditation demands that we overcome the misconception that awareness as such – what is called pure awareness – is something that is 'ours', that is 'yours' or 'mine' – and thus the personal property of our ego or 'I'.

To enter a true state of *meditative* awareness however – to 'meditate' – is the opposite of 'I-dentifying' with any thing or things we are aware of.

> *To meditate is to give ourselves time to identify*
> *with the pure awareness of what is going on –*
> *and not with any element or aspect of it.*

That is why the truly aware person on the other hand, does not think '*I* think this' or '*I* feel that', '*I* recall this' or '*I* would like that'. Instead, were it put into words, their *experience* of awareness would not begin with the word 'I' but with the words 'There is..'. They would not think to themselves '*I* think this' or 'I feel that' but rather '*There is an awareness* in me of this thought' or '*There is an awareness* in me of this feeling'. Thus they would not think 'I feel tired' or 'I feel anxious' but rather '*There is an awareness* of tiredness in me' or '*There is an awareness* of anxiety in me'. This is important, because the foundation of all meditation is the understanding that the awareness of a thought or feeling, mood or emotion, impulse or activity, need or desire, *is not itself* a thought or feeling, mood or emotion, impulse or activity, need or desire, but is instead something innately free of all these elements of our experiencing. For just as our awareness of a thing such as a table is not itself a thing, not itself a table, so is our awareness of a thought not itself a thought. Instead it is something innately thought free. Thus we do not need to effortfully 'empty', 'clear' or 'free' our mind of thoughts in order to reach a state of pure thought-free awareness. On the contrary, all we need do is identify with the pure awareness of our thoughts. The same applies to all elements of our experience, all so-called contents of consciousness. We do not need to empty our consciousness of these contents in order to achieve a state of awareness free of attachment to them. For the simple awareness of those contents is itself an awareness free from and unattached to them.

Meditation then, is based on the recognition that awareness as such – pure awareness – is not bound or restricted to any particular thing or things we are aware *of* – whether in the form of thoughts or feelings, impulses or sensations, needs or desires, memories or anticipations. Instead, it is like *space* – for though space is inseparable from the objects in it, it also remains absolutely distinct from them, and is not itself any 'thing'. Pure awareness, quite simply, is a clear and empty space *of* awareness – for whilst it embraces everything we experience, it remains absolutely distinct from each and every element of our experience, each and every 'thing' we are aware *of*.

To not get lost, stressed, drained, depressed or fatigued by whatever is going on – whatever we might be doing or saying, thinking or feeling – demands only that we stop identifying with the immediate *focus* of our awareness and identify instead with the larger space or *field* of awareness around it. What we ordinarily call 'consciousness' is a type of highly focused or focal awareness. True *awareness* on the other hand is a type of non-focal, non-local or *field consciousness*. As long as people are identified with the immediate focus of their awareness whether external or internal, they remain as if *encapsulated* in a bubble from which no amount of social interaction and communication will free them – for all this allows them is the relief of *self-expression* of whatever it is they are aware of from within their respective bubbles. Paradoxically, freedom from such encapsulation in ourselves and in what we think of as 'our' awareness can be attained only by granting more awareness to our most *fleshly* capsule – our skin – using it to sense the larger space *around* our heads and bodies. For that larger space is in essence but a larger field or space *of awareness*. It is by identifying with this larger space that we identify with the *pure awareness* of all that is going on – whether within or between our own 'bubbles' of awareness and those of others.

Expanding our *awareness of space* then, is the key to *experiencing* awareness itself *as* an expansive, all-embracing and transcendent space – embracing and transcending not just our own body but that of every thing and person within it. By sensing and identifying with an expanded awareness of space, we cease to experience awareness as something encapsulated in our minds or brains or bounded by our own skin.

To truly be *aware* is to literally be *in* awareness – to experience ourselves abiding or dwelling within a spacious field of pure awareness in the same way as our bodies abide and dwell within space. That spacious expanse of the pure awareness in which we all dwell is not 'ours', not 'yours' nor 'mine', and yet it is the very essence of the divine. For as it is written in the Bhagavad Gita:

As the mighty Air that pervades everything ever abides in Space, know that in the same way all Beings abide in Me.

We all seek 'breathing space' in our busy lives. To 'meditate' is to identify with *the pure awareness* of all that is going on. This means sensing and identifying with the larger field or *space* within which it goes on. In this way we begin to feel more *breathing* space – not by breathing fresh air or by doing exercises in 'breath control' but by literally breathing in the very 'air-ness' of pure awareness itself – that 'higher air' or 'aether' which pervades all things, yet abides in the seeming emptiness of the space around them.

To begin with however, all we need 'do' to meditate is to give ourselves time to grant full awareness to our *bodies* – allowing ourselves to be as fully aware as possible of any elements of anxiety, stress, tension, restlessness or dis-ease, however subtle or intense, that we sense within them. By giving awareness to our bodies in this way, we can, at the same time, give time to become more aware of things going on in our lives that may be 'on our mind' or that 'come to mind' as conscious mental thoughts or concerns directly related to what we are feeling in our bodies. The longer we do this, the more time we give ourselves *to be aware* – first of all of our bodies as a whole and then of all that preoccupies our minds – the more we will sense a gap opening up between our body-mind and the everyday self it constitutes and the very awareness we are granting it. In this way we begin to feel a gap between our everyday self and identity and another deep self – that Self which is *granting awareness* to our everyday self and lives, that Self, which, in its essence *is* the awareness we are granting.

When we begin to sense that second, deeper Self we take the second major step in meditation. If the first step is giving ourselves time to be aware, the second is passing from 'being aware' to 'being awareness'. This means ceasing to identify with anything we are aware *of* in our bodies and minds, but identifying instead with that very *awareness* we are giving ourselves, and with the Self that *is* that awareness, our 'awareness self' (the 'Atman').

Feeling that Self 'immanently' – from deep down inside or within our bodies – we can then begin to feel it 'transcendentally'. This is the third stage of meditation. We reach it by giving awareness not just to all that is going on inside us – in the inner spaces of our bodies and within our minds – but also to our skin surface, using it to sense more intensely the clear empty space surrounding our heads and bodies. As we expand our awareness into that space we begin to feel it as an infinite space *of* awareness – of which not just our body but all bodies are but different shapes or expressions. All that we were previously more intensely aware of as 'going' on in our body and mind – indeed in our everyday life in its entirety – we now experience as nothing more than shallow ripples and reflections on the surface of a fathomless, underground ocean of awareness. At the same time, we feel the deeper Self within us as one centre of a vast, vaulting *time-space* of awareness – one that spans our entire lifetime.

It is *as and from* this Self that we can give ourselves time to 'meditate' at any time, simply by giving more awareness to all that is going on within us or pre-occupying our bodies and minds – whilst at the same time 'breathing' the pure air or 'aether' of that clear, contentless awareness which surrounds us as space itself, and that spans all of time.

Basic Meditational Awareness Practices

The Primary Practice of Awareness (1)

1. Without closing your eyes, take time to be aware of all there is to be aware of both within and around you – impulses, sensations, emotions and thoughts within you; the air, light, objects and space around you.

2. Attend particularly to your wordless, bodily awareness of all these things – where and how you sense them with and within your body. For example, be aware of the inner voice you hear speaking thoughts in your head, of the inner ear with which you hear them, and different sensual textures and qualities of your bodily self-awareness.

3. Concentrate on sensing *where* you feel particular mental states, moods or emotions with and within your body and *how* – which is not *as* mental-emotional states but as purely *sensual* textures and qualities of your bodily self-experience.

4. Remind yourself that the awareness of an object, sensation, emotion or thought is not *itself* an object, sensation, emotion or thought – that it is innately *free* of all objects, sensations, emotions and thoughts. For awareness as such is both inseparable and absolutely distinct from all we are aware of.

5. With this mantra or reminder in mind do not identify with anything in particular that you are aware *of* – but rather with the simple, pure *awareness* of it. Feel how this pure awareness embraces and transcends everything you are aware of – in just the same way that the space around you embraces and yet transcends every thing within it.

6. Sense the very space, light and air around you as a pure space, light and air *of* awareness – one that permeates every atom and cell of your body and pervades the physical space around it. Sense yourself breathing in the pure space, light and air of awareness through every pore of your skin and into a hollow space in your diaphragm – the heart of the divine awareness within you.

7. Sense your whole body and self as nothing but a manifestation of the space around it – of the pure space, light and air of awareness itself. Remind yourself that this is the divine source of your being, your body and of everything and everyone you are aware of within and around you. Thus, experiencing your body and self as an expression of the divine awareness you unite or 'join' with it – the meaning of 'yoga' and the aim of yoga meditation.

The Primary Practice of Awareness (2)

1. Close your eyes, and simply feel the fleshly, physical warmth pervading your body.

2. Now take time to simply be aware of all the muscles you are using to breathe – those of your ribcage, back, diaphragm and abdomen. Through them feel how deep or shallow, rapid or slow your breathing is – and let it be that way. Do not wilfully alter your breathing in any way unless or until a spontaneous bodily impulse to do so arises.

3. Now take time to grant awareness to different areas of your inwardly felt body. In particular any regions of your body where you have any sense of dis-ease or discomfort, whether in the form of a muscular tension, emotional anxiety or discomfort, fatigue or over-fullness, dullness or density.

4. Staying aware of your breathing, and taking time to grant awareness to different regions of your body in turn, allow yourself to feel how in doing so it is as if you are inwardly airing your body with awareness, so that its felt inner space begins to feel purified, clear and translucent.

5. Be aware too of any thoughts, recollections, images or concepts that arise in your mind whilst meditating. Remind yourself that any moods, emotions or sensations you are aware of in your body are in turn an awareness of something to do with your personal life and world as a whole. Meditating your immediate bodily self-awareness, let whatever it calls to mind in relation to your life world as a whole come to mind.

6. Allow yourself to regularly return your awareness to any regions of your body wherever you still feel a sense of dis-ease, until the awareness itself begins to dissipate it, letting the manner of your breathing change in any way you feel helpful.

7. Opening your eyes, help this dissipation, clearing and clearing process by now becoming more aware of your body as a whole, using your whole body surface to sense the air and space around you, and any scents or sounds in it.

8. Sustaining this awareness of your body and sensing the space and air around it, meditate on feeling your whole body – and every aspect of your self that you experience within it – as a manifestation of that surrounding air and space.

9. Do not identify with any thoughts, images, emotions or bodily sensations but with the pure awareness of them and feel this pure awareness as the very space around them, distinct from and yet embracing and manifesting as everything within it, including your own body.

10. Feel the clear light, space and air of pure awareness pervading the spaces of every atom, molecule and cell of your body as you breathe. In this way begin to feel your breathing as a breathing of the pure air or aether of awareness through every pore of your skin.

11. Breathing entirely with your abdominal muscles, be aware in particular of the region of your lower abdomen, and feel yourself breathing awareness into a hollow space within it. Sense a silent, still-point of awareness in your abdomen, a couple of inches below and behind the navel, and actively centre both your breathing and awareness in it.

12. Sense your body as a whole as nothing bounded by your flesh or body surface but as boundless space of awareness with and surround it. Sense awareness itself *as* space, light and air – and also as the simple feeling of warmth and fluid warmth of feeling filling the safe containing womb of your flesh.

Meditation, Movement and 'Just Sitting'

'Meditation', as understood through The Awareness Principle, means simply giving *time-space* to a type of wholly non-active or 'quiescent' awareness – one not reliant on bodily movement or action. Most Westerners however, can only feel a sense of meditative inner stillness through movement in space.

Sitting still, they can no longer feel their body as a whole, let alone sense the space of awareness, around it – but instead begin to get lost in thought and their heads. Put in other terms, they cannot sustain a 'proprioceptive' awareness of their own body without sensations of physical movement – without 'kinaesthetic' awareness.

That is why they need to be constantly 'on the move' – whether through any type of physical activity involving movement of the body, or by literally moving from place to place – for example by travelling or engaging in pursuits such as walking, jogging, swimming etc.

That is also why a notable guru of the nineteen sixties and seventies felt forced to come up with the idea of so-called 'dynamic meditation' – effectively no form of meditation at all but a mere means of emotional catharsis through spontaneous movement.

Kinaesthetic awareness – dependent on movement – does indeed awaken proprioceptive awareness. Yet in Western culture it is, for most people, the *only* way they know of awakening or sustaining proprioceptive awareness of their bodies.

In Eastern and aboriginal cultures the reverse has been traditionally the case – movement and *kinaesthetic* awareness are grounded in motionless stillness and *proprioceptive* awareness of one's body.

As in the practice of Tai Chi and of different forms of Asian dance and martial art, Eastern cultures value forms of bodily movement which arise out of a sense of motionless stillness – and believe in letting this very motionless stillness guide and time their physical movement or 'kinesis'. Thus the most truly advanced martial artist is precisely one who does not actively move their body at all, but rather lets it *be moved* – moved by a 'proprioceptive' awareness that embraces not only their body but their sense of the entire space around their body.

It is because the 'kinaesthetic' awareness of the martial artist is *already* so highly trained that all they require to guide their physical movements is a meditative, motionless proprioceptive awareness.

Sitting meditation on the other hand, teaches people how to 'move' in a different way – to move from one location or 'place' to another *in themselves* – not with their physical body but *within* their inwardly felt body.

Strictly speaking this is not movement at all but *awareness* – awareness of the many different sensations and feelings and thoughts that are presencing or *occurring* in different regions or locations of their body. It is awareness too, of the relation of these sensations or feelings, whether subtle or intense, to the thoughts they are having and to the things or people they are connected with in their world.

The principle aim of sitting meditation is to learn how to be physically still whilst still sustaining awareness of our body as a whole and the space around it – sustaining both proprioceptive and spatial awareness.

This proprioceptive awareness is what sitting meditation and the Zen practice of 'just sitting' was implicitly designed to cultivate. Yet the problems faced by students of Zen-style sitting meditation – physical restlessness, mental boredom or drifting off, were not understood and responded to with this understanding or aim in mind – the aim of cultivating awareness of our bodies and the space around them.

Instead they were left to struggle with sensations of restlessness, strain, boredom or fatigue leading them to mentally dissociate from their bodies rather than become more aware of them, to get lost in thought or even fall asleep during meditation – hence the Master's 'awakening' stick. There was no instruction to students to fully *affirm* all bodily sensations in awareness – thus coming to recognise that the very *awareness* of a bodily sensation is not itself anything bodily but is essentially *bodiless* and *sensation-free*.

Similarly the *awareness* of a distracting thought or mental state is not itself anything mental or any activity of mind – 'mindfulness' – but is instead something essentially *thought- and mind-free*.

Lacking this understanding and experience of pure awareness, Zen students were left to rely on their minds to distract or dissociate themselves from their bodies – or to simply stay awake. This however only compounded the challenge of attaining a state of pure, mind- and thought-free awareness.

What they required was 'The Awareness Principle' – the recognition that just as the awareness of our bodies and of bodily sensations is not itself anything bodily, so is the pure awareness of our minds and thoughts not itself anything mental but a thought and mind-free awareness.

The Zen *practice* of sitting meditation aimed at transcending both mind and body and attaining a state called emptiness or *mu* – 'No mind. No body.' Yet this practice did not recognise that the pure *awareness* of mind and body is – *in principle* – something innately transcendent or free of body and mind.

Without this recognition, 'success' in meditation came to be identified more and more with 'one-pointedness' – the *concentration* of awareness on a single inner or outer focal point (for example the centre of a *mandala*.). It is precisely this practice of 'one-pointedness' however, that *misses the point* – which is that a state of pure mind- and body-free awareness is, in contrast to ordinary consciousness, precisely an awareness *not* focussed or concentrated on a single, localised point. Instead it is an all-round 'field' awareness embracing the entirety of space – not least the space around our bodies, around our physical sensations and around our thoughts themselves.

It is from the *formless all-round space of pure awareness* that all formed elements of our bodily and mental experiencing, inner and outer, arise. To concentrate 'single-pointedly' on any one of these is to miss the central aim of meditation, which is to cultivate a proprioceptive *awareness* of our bodies – and even our thoughts themselves – from the space surrounding them.

The term 'sacred space' is both true and misleading. For a sacred space or a holy place such as a temple or cathedral, is in essence any place which helps us – either through its vast inner or outer dimensions and/or through its association with God or the divine – to experience space as such *as* sacred and holy – *as* the divine and *as* the God inside which we dwell.

What happens when people enter a sacred space such as a large cathedral for example is – first of all – that they gain a sense of its vaulting spaciousness, and at the same time, by virtue of knowing the cathedral as a holy place or 'house of God' – associate this spaciousness with that holiness and with God.

When people come together in temples, churches or mosques they are first of all aware of being together in a common space which is recognised as sacred or holy in some way. In that way, they knowingly or unknowingly come to an experience of space itself as divine – that which embraces all things and beings. *Going* to a holy place involves movement in space. Yet *being there* means motionlessly abiding in that place, thus coming to experiencing its space – and thereby space itself – as holy.

Again, movement or *kinesis* – activity or change of place – can be a way of awakening or sustaining proprioceptive awareness, or it can be a way of avoiding it. Yet the question whether, at any given moment, awareness is better sustained through movement or non-movement, can itself only be decided by first of all *not*-moving – by abiding in a motionless stillness.

Mountains and trees do not move from place to place, go to church, go for walks or go on pilgrimages. Mountains will not come to Mohammed. Trees do not have eyes to see. Yet they are the true '*Zen* masters' and *yogis* of nature. For not having eyes to perceive space or limbs by which to move from place to place, they are masters at motionlessly sensing the space, light and air around them. Indeed their proprioceptive sense of their own bodies comes from sensing their spatiality.

The tree's trunk rises towards the heights of the sky. Its roots plumb the depths of the earth. Its branches spread and its leaves and flowers open themselves to the vaulting curvature of the heavens above – absorbing the light and air of space not through any eyes or noses, but through their *entire surface*.

To be 'conscious' is to be aware of things occurring – abiding or moving – 'in' the space around them. To be *aware* of things however, is not the same as to *be* that very awareness. To *be* awareness means to *be* the space, inner and outer, in which things occur, and not just be aware of things occurring in that space. For pure awareness, in our space-time reality, *is* space. Being *space*, we do not need to engage in activity or movement to experience *time*. For space is *time-space*. The vaulting expanse of space *is* the spacious expanse of time itself – a time-space that embraces all actions and places – past, present and future – without any need for movement from one place to another 'in' space or one moment to another 'in' time.

Practicing Sitting as Meditation

Sitting meditation is essentially the experience of sitting – anywhere and anytime – *as* meditation. This involves 4 simple steps:

1. Sitting with your eyes open, but not looking at anything.

2. Sustaining awareness of your sensed body surface as a whole.

3. Feeling your body surface as 'all eye' – enabling you to sense the entire space within and all around your body.

4. Letting all that you are aware of within your body in the form of sensations or feelings and all that comes to mind in the form of thoughts and images dissipate into the space around your body.

Bodily and Spatial Awareness

The most fundamental Practice of Awareness is the practice of sustaining continuous 'whole-body awareness' throughout the day. The foundation of this whole-body awareness is awareness of one's felt body surface as a whole. For without awareness of our surface we can feel neither the inner *space of awareness* it bounds and surrounds nor the awareness that *is the outer* space surrounding it – these being the two distinct but inseparable aspects of the 'awareness space' that make up our 'awareness body' or 'soul body'. Surface awareness is thus the key to experiencing 'whole-body' awareness as 'soul-body' awareness. Sustaining this whole-body/soul-body awareness through spatial body awareness can only be achieved through constant mindfulness and regular recall of the following twelve questions – all of which have to do and affect how much space one feels one has – both for oneself and for others.

Meditating Awareness as Space

1. How much of my body surface am I feeling right now?
2. How much inner awareness space can I feel within this felt surface boundary?
3. Where do I feel my awareness concentrated in this inner awareness space?
4. Where do I feel my awareness centred in this inner-bodily awareness space?
5. How far down does my inner awareness space extend from the inner space of my head through that of my chest to my lower abdomen?
6. How expansive or contracted, crowded or empty, muddied or clear, do I feel the inner awareness space of my head, chest and abdomen?
7. To what extent do I feel the inner awareness space of head, chest and abdomen as a singular inner space of awareness?
8. To what extent can I lower my centre of awareness from a point in my head to points in the inner region of my heart, diaphragm, belly and lower abdomen?
9. To what extent can I sense the entire space around my body surface?
10. How far can I feel my awareness extending into this space?
11. To what extent can I feel the entire space around me as an unbounded space of awareness enveloping and embracing both my own body and every other body in it?
12. How permeable or impermeable do I feel the surface boundary between my inner and outer awareness spaces – to what extent can I feel my surface boundary as either a porous in-breathing membrane or as a sealed self-containing boundary?

Expanding Spatial Awareness

Note: this meditation is to be practiced in the true *tantric* manner – attending to your 'inner space' but with your eyes still open. This is so that you can stay aware of the entire space around you ('Bhairava Mudra'), expanding your awareness into that space and experiencing everything in it as an expression of it. This practice of Khechari Mudra – uniting the Kingdom outside with the Kingdom inside – is the key to all the miraculous 'Siddhis' exercised by great Yogis, Gurus and Avatars.

1. Bring your awareness to the inwardly sensed surface of your chest and body as a whole. From that surface sense the empty spaces in front of, above, behind and to either side of your body.

2. Attend entirely to your awareness of regions of empty space – those above and around your body, and those above, around and between other bodily objects or people.

3. Be aware of the sky above and of the unlimited expanse of cosmic space, and of all empty regions of space in your immediate vicinity or scope of vision.

4. Sense all regions of 'empty' space as part of an unlimited space of pure awareness – a space totally untainted by any psychical qualities, be they the 'atmosphere' of places, the 'aura' of people and the mood or 'space' you or others may feel themselves in.

5. Feel your body surface again, this time sensing a hollow space of pure awareness within it – a space equally untainted by any thoughts, feelings or sensations you experience within it.

6. Identify with the spaces of awareness around and between all that you experience outside and inside you – the space around and between your thoughts, emotions and physical sensations, the space around and between your body and other bodies.

7. Attend to your breathing, and feel yourself breathing in the luminous translucency of the space around you, first through your chest and body surface as a whole – experiencing this as a breathing of pure awareness.

8. Feel your chest and body surface as an open, porous, in-breathing skin or membrane uniting a content-free space of pure awareness within you with the 'empty' space of pure awareness surrounding your own body and all other bodies.

Aspects of the Practice of Awareness

1. BEING AWARE

Taking all the time necessary to be aware of all you are experiencing inwardly and outwardly, and of every distinct element of your experiencing, from thoughts and feelings, to somatic sensations and every element of your sensory environment.

2. BODILY AWARENESS

Attending to the immediate bodily dimension of all that you are aware of experiencing – where and how you feel different things you perceive or are aware of in an immediate sensual, proprioceptive and bodily way.

3. BODYING AWARENESS

Giving some form of authentic bodily expression to your awareness, for example through your posture, the tilt of your body or head, the look on your face or in your eyes, the tone or tempo of your voice – thus amplifying, bodying and silently communicating your awareness of it.

4. UNBOUNDING YOUR AWARENESS

Reminding yourself that your bodily awareness of your body is not itself bounded by your body, but is an unbounded bodiless awareness that permeates your body, all of space and every body in it.

5. BEING-IN-AWARENESS

You dwell IN awareness as you dwell in space itself. Being-in-Awareness is a way of Being Awareness, by not identifying with what you are aware of, but identifying instead with the very spaces of awareness, inner and outer, *in* which you experience them.

6. BREATHING AWARENESS

Expanding the 'breathing space' of your awareness by giving yourself time to be aware of the way you are – or are not – breathing, by shifting your awareness TO your breathing, and experiencing it as a breathing OF awareness – feeling yourself breathing your awareness of the entire sensory space around you through your chest surface, felt as open and porous.

7. BEING AWARENESS

Being-in, Bodying and Breathing awareness are paths that lead from Being Aware to Being Awareness. Being Awareness means affirming and feeling the meaningfulness of all that you are aware of, whilst not identifying with it but instead identifying with the very awareness of it – BEING that awareness instead of BINDING your awareness to what you are aware of. To BE awareness is to be the all-round SPACE, inner and outer, in which you experience things – including your own body. To identify with AWARENESS as such is to identify with SPACE as such.

8. UNBINDING AWARENESS

Each time you become aware of experiencing something new, step back once again into Being Awareness in order to

UNBIND your awareness from it – thus continuing both to Be Aware and to Be Awareness rather than letting your awareness become BOUND by anything you are aware of.

9. BEING-IN-AWARENESS WITH OTHERS

Relating in a meditative way by using every encounter as an opportunity to give yourself time to Be Aware of others, to Breathe in your awareness of them, and to feel the space around you both as a space of awareness in which you can both 'Be in Awareness' together.

10. ATTAINING AWARENESS BLISS

The bliss that arises from recognising that you are not a being with awareness but that you ARE awareness – part of the unbounded awareness that IS 'God'. Awareness Bliss is only attained through Being Aware, Being and Bodying Awareness, Breathing Awareness, and Being in Awareness with others, – breathing the divine awareness that both you and others are.

The Primary Mantra of Awareness

1. Be aware whenever you find yourself thinking or saying to yourself or others 'I *am*...'. For example, 'I *am*... lonely/depressed/anxious/afraid/trapped/bitter/worthless/ angry/frustrated/resentful/ashamed/unworthy/ugly/unloved/ bad/mad, a failure etc. Fill in the blank dots following the words 'I am ...' with whatever words fit your sense of how you 'are'.

2. Now replace the word *am* with the words 'feel' or 'think' and say to yourself 'I *feel* ... and *think* I am ...' [fill in your own words].

3. Remind yourself that you *are not* your feelings or thoughts about yourself - that thoughts and feelings *about* reality *are not* reality.

4. Now seek to follow the words 'I feel...' or 'I think...' with a description of *where and how* you sense the feeling or emotion in your body. Example: "I feel a fluttering in my chest which makes me think I am 'anxious'."

5. Now give yourself time to be aware of how you sense and feel your body *as a whole* and the space around it – rather than focussing on any localised thoughts emotions or sensations felt within it.

6. In order not to *identify* with your feelings and thoughts, remove the word 'I'. Rather than saying to yourself 'I am...', 'I feel ...', or 'I think ...' say to yourself '*There is an awareness* of being/thinking/feeling ...' Again, seek to describe how you 'are' as a bodily sensation, and return to feeling your body as a whole.

7. Make it a rule to say to yourself '*There is an awareness* of ....' instead of 'I am...', 'I feel...' or 'I think...' For example "*There is an awareness* of thinking or feeling 'X'." For ultimately it is not any 'I' but IT – *awareness as such* – that thinks, feels, perceives and experiences all things. 'Not "I" but IT – awareness – experiences this' – that is 'The Primary Mantra' of The Awareness Principle.

Part 3

Counselling, Meditation and Yoga

What is 'meditation'? And is there such a thing as a 'yogic' or 'meditational' approach to both counselling and psychotherapy?

The term 'Non-Dual Therapy' has now established itself as a type of umbrella term for approaches to counselling and therapy rooted in yogic philosophy and incorporating both a spiritual or 'trans-personal' dimension and meditational practices of different sorts.

First a word about words and terms. The term 'meditation', though it is of course associated with Eastern spiritual traditions, is not itself an Eastern word but a European one. It derives from the Latin words *mederi* (to give attention or awareness to something or someone) and *meditari* (to reflect, study on or apply oneself to something). It is commonly used to translate the Sanskrit term *Sadhana* – meaning 'to practice'.

The expression 'non-dual' is a direct and literal translation of the Sanskrit term *Advaita*. 'Non-duality' or *Advaita* are terms closely related in meaning with the word 'yoga' itself – which means 'union' and derives from the Indo-European root *ieug* (to join or yoke together).

Advaita or 'non-dualism' (*A-dvaita*) is also the name and the basic principle of an important school of Indian 'yogic' philosophy, aimed at distinguishing it from so-called 'dualistic' or *Dvaita* schools. It is this basic principle that I have rethought, refined and redefined – calling it simply 'The Awareness Principle'.

What is the essence of 'non-duality' (*Advaita*) or 'union' (*yoga*)? In my understanding it is not just 'one-ness' as opposed to duality or 'two-ness', 'union' as opposed to separation – for this would constitute a *dualistic* opposition in itself. Instead the essence of both 'union' and 'non-duality' can best be seen as a relation of *inseparable distinction*. An example is the relation between two sides of the same coin or sheet of paper – which are both distinct (and therefore dual) but also absolutely inseparable (and therefore non-dual).

In the development of Advaitic or non-dual philosophy itself, it was acknowledged that to see non-duality and duality as opposing or *dual* concepts would run against the very principle of *non*-duality. Only a new understanding of unity or non-duality as a relation of 'inseparable distinction' can fully clarify what, in the *Advaitic* tradition itself, was called 'the non-duality of duality and non-duality'.

Another example of 'non-duality' as 'inseparable distinction' is the relation of empty space to the objects in it. For space is both inseparable from everything in it and yet at the same time distinct from it.

Yet what have these abstract philosophical terms and concepts to do with counselling? The most important thing to understand is that, unlike yogic practices and the philosophy of non-dualism, no Western *psychology* or form of counselling has any concept of a type of *pure awareness* which – like space – is both inseparable and yet absolutely distinct from everything we experience within it – whether outer perceptions, or inwardly experienced moods and sensations, needs and impulses, thoughts and emotions.

The Western 'psychological' understanding (and experience) of the soul or *psyche* is a sort of internal space of awareness inside our head or bodies and bounded by them. Yet most people neither sense the insideness of their bodies nor the space around them as a space of clear uncluttered awareness. Instead they may either feel 'empty' in a depressed way, or else as brimful of impulses and sensations, thoughts and emotions, voices and mental images, memories, impulses and other elements of experience to the point of 'overwhelm'. It is such elements of their experiencing which so pre-occupy the *space* of people's inner and outer worlds that they derive their whole sense of *self* from them – whilst at the same time leaving them quite literally with a sense of having no 'space' for themselves or for significant others.

The aim of Advaitic philosophy and yogic meditational practice is to find that space and in doing so feel a quite different self to the one that has 'no space' for itself or others. This is a self that is able to feel *space itself* as a realm of pure awareness distinct and free from anything experienced within it.

This self is not the everyday personal self we are aware of. It is not even a self that can be said to 'have' or 'possess' awareness. Instead it is that Self which *is* awareness. The idea of a Self that is identical with awareness *as such* is not my invention. For one of the important yogic treatises or *tantra* – the 'Shiva Sutras'– declares as its opening statement or sutra that 'Awareness *is* the Self'.

This Self, which I term 'The Awareness Self', was called *Atman*, *Chaitanya* or *Chaitanyatman*. It was understood as 'non-dual' – as inseparable from a universal soul or ultimate and divine awareness (*Anuttara*). Identifying with *this* Self was understood as a way of freeing or liberating ourselves from identification with a much more limited self – that self which is wholly identified or bound up with whatever is currently going on, whatever we are currently doing or saying, whatever we are currently focussing our awareness on – or whatever is preoccupying the inner and outer spaces of our awareness. That is why in another famous treatise – the *Vijnanabhairava Tantra* – identification with the apparent emptiness of space was seen as a key to the ultimate aim of yoga – freedom or *Moksha*. By this was meant freedom from a self-limiting identification with anything we happen to be experiencing or aware *of*.

Now this distinction between a liberated or unbound self and a bound or limited self, between that self which *is* awareness and any self we are aware *of* – has profound significance in the context of counselling and therapy. Why? Because whilst the aim of counselling is to help people get 'clearer' about troubling experiences and emotions, and in this way to also 'free' them from them, the aim is a difficult if not impossible one to achieve if a client's whole *sense of self* is identified and bound up with their suffering – if not wholly dependent on it.

The vital role that yoga has to play in counselling is to show how it is possible to identify and achieve union with the 'Awareness Self' – that self which does not 'have' but *is* awareness.

Learning to identify with space itself, inner and outer, as pure awareness and thereby uniting with that Self which is awareness – this is 'yoga' in the truest sense. At its heart is what I term 'The Awareness Principle', which together with the many 'Practices of Awareness' that go with it, constitute what I call 'The New Yoga of Awareness'.

Teaching this New Yoga to counselling clients requires first of all that counsellors themselves learn what is perhaps the most basic Principle and Practice of Awareness. This is the principle and practice of distinguishing between each and every thing we are *aware of* (whether within or around us, positive or negative, painful or pleasurable) from the *pure awareness* of it – from awareness *as such*.

To engage in this Practice of Awareness it is helpful, if not vital, to remind ourselves of the basic relation between pure awareness and 'empty' space. A simple way of helping someone to understand this relation is to request that they look around and name any tangible thing they are aware of around them – a wall painting, computer, chair or desk for example – and then to put to them the following simple questions: "Is *the awareness* of that thing itself a 'thing' of any sort?" For example: "Is *the awareness* of a painting, computer, desk or chair *itself* a painting, computer, desk or chair?"

The point that such questions can help to get over is that *awareness* of an object in the space around us is not itself an object 'in' space. Instead awareness *is* the very space in which any object is perceived. Your outer awareness of a table for example is not *itself* a table, but the space in which you perceive it. Similarly, the inner awareness of a sensation, thought or emotion is *not itself* a sensation, thought or emotion. Instead it is the inner *space* within which the sensation, thought or emotion is experienced. The same basic Principle of Awareness in other words, applies to any and all 'elements' of our experience, inner and outer – showing that awareness *as such* is distinct from all of them.

Since the awareness of a thought, for example, *is not itself a thought*, awareness as such is something innately *thought-free* – just as it is also innately free of each and every element of our experience.

Consequently – and yet in contrast to how many actual or would-be practitioners of meditation see it – to achieve a meditative state of pure 'thought-free' awareness does not require any effort at all; does not require us to 'clear' or 'free' our minds of thoughts. All that is required is to identify with the already clear and thought-free space of awareness *within which* we experience any thought.

Coming to rest within a space of pure awareness is the essence of *meditation*. That is why 'meditation' – as long as it is clearly understood as a practice of *awareness* and not merely a practice of walking or sitting in a certain way – is the central link between counselling and yoga. Yet though the terms 'meditation' and 'yoga' are commonly used, their meaning is rarely considered or defined in such a precise way. Only in this way however, can their value for counsellors and their clients become apparent.

In what I call 'The New Yoga' – the yoga of *awareness* – 'yoga' does not mean sitting alone or in class with people and effortfully adopting different bodily postures or engaging in stretching exercises. Nor does 'meditation' mean effortfully attempting to empty your mind in expectation of some undefined state of 'enlightenment'. It is not 'just sitting' but 'just being aware' – sitting with the simple intent to give ourselves *time to be aware*. Giving ourselves *time* to be aware allows us to become much *more* aware than we usually are of all that is going on within and around us. This in turn allows us to do three important things:

Firstly, it allows us to *identify and distinguish* much more clearly all the different elements of our immediate experiencing such as moods, sensations, memories, thoughts emotions etc.

Secondly it allow us to *fully acknowledge, feel and affirm* each and every element of our immediate experiencing – whether pleasurable or painful, mental, emotional or somatic.

Last but not least, it allows us to distinguish each and every element of our current experience from the pure awareness of it, and to feel that very awareness as a clear space in which we can feel independent and free of anything we experience or are aware of.

Sometimes people confuse dis-identification with 'detaching' ourselves from our feelings and other elements of our experience. This is a misunderstanding. For meditation begins with freely choosing to *feel* our feelings – and all elements of our experience – more fully and not less. To *feel and affirm* a particular mood, sensation, desire, emotion or thought is by no means the same thing as *identifying* with that element of our experience. Indeed it is the very opposite of doing so. For freely choosing to become more aware of something is itself the very first step to identifying with pure awareness as such. And it is by giving ourselves time to feel and follow any element of our experience that it will transform – revealing itself to *be an awareness* of something beyond it. A sensation, emotion or thought for example, is not only something we are aware *of*. It is itself the expression *of* an awareness, for example in the form of a new insight into a particular situation, possibility or person.

To follow our experiences to this point of transformation, as well as reaching a state of identification with *pure awareness* takes time however, which is why the defining principle and practice of meditation – giving ourselves *time* to be aware – is so important.

For we know also that in today's globalised Western culture people are driven to occupy their time with everything *but* awareness – to keep themselves permanently preoccupied and busy with different activities. The result of this culture of busy-ness is that people keep their awareness so filled up and preoccupied that they end up feeling no space for themselves – or no self to feel. This in turn makes them more addicted to activities, mental-emotional states, behaviours or experiences which – whether habitual or compulsive, mundane or 'extreme', pleasurable or painful, normal or pathological – can serve to bestow or restore a sense of self.

It is significant too, that in everyday English – itself a global language – the phrases 'don't have time for' and 'don't have space for...' or 'wish I had more time for..' and 'wish I had more space for...' are used synonymously. This not having space for things or people – not to mention oneself – comes about through not meditating, through not giving ourselves *time* to just be aware. Conversely however, giving ourselves that time to be aware is what gives us a sense of having more *space*.

This brings us to another reason why people would rather *not* give themselves time to be aware – and instead see even such things as counselling, meditation and yoga as just other things to 'do' or 'experience', other ways of 'using' or 'filling' time. The reason I refer to is *fear* – the fear that if they did truly meditate, if they *did* give themselves more time to be aware and *did* feel more space as a result, they might feel that space as totally empty – a black hole, void or vacuum devoid of any self at all, rather than as a space of pure, liberating awareness. For this is a space distinct from all the things that normally preoccupy us and yet expansive enough to embrace them in such a way that we no longer feel stressed or overwhelmed by them. It is a space in which we can feel even our ordinary limited experience of ourselves safely held – yet one that is at the same time big enough to 'make room' for others – and for *new* experiences of ourselves and the world around us. 'Meditation' means entering this expanded SPACE of awareness by giving ourselves more TIME to be aware.

Many people have been introduced to or practiced different forms of 'meditation'. What follows is a description of some basic stages of meditation based on the precise definition of it given above – as a practice of giving ourselves *time to be aware* and in this way expanding the *space* of awareness in which we can dwell – not just whilst meditating but throughout our everyday lives.

1. To begin with, take time to look around and become more aware of the different elements of your *outer experiencing* – for example the different features of the people and objects in this room. Now take time to be aware of the clear space surrounding everything and everybody in this room, not just the space you can see in front of you but the space as you can sense it both in front of you and behind you, above you and to either side of you. Sense this clear space not just as an empty space surrounding the things and people you are aware of but as a clear space *of* awareness, one without which you could not be aware of anything or anybody within it.

2. The next stage is to close your eyes, turn your gaze inwards with your inner eye and take time to be more aware of the different elements of your inner experiencing. To begin with, just sense the interiority or insideness of different regions of your body – whether head, chest, belly or abdomen. Sense each of these regions of your body as if it were a hollow space. If you can, feel these hollow spaces of head, chest, belly and abdomen as one singular space or hollow of awareness bounded by your body.

Now take two or three minutes to become *more aware*, one by one, of the different types of thing you can sense yourself experiencing within these spaces – for example the tone and 'colour' of your overall mood, subtle bodily sensations and tensions, thoughts and feelings about your yourself and others etc. Allow yourself also to be aware, in the present, of thoughts and feelings arising from recollections of recent events and experiences or anticipations of future ones. Most importantly, if you are or become aware of any sense of dis-ease, of any discomforting thoughts, feelings or sensations, do all of the following three things:

- Firstly give them more awareness – all the awareness they are asking for.

- Secondly, remind yourself that the very awareness of a thought, feeling or sensation is not itself a thought, feeling or sensation.

- Thirdly, whenever you sense yourself identifying with any discomforting thoughts, feelings or sensation, remind yourself to identify instead with the space or spaces of awareness within which you experience them.

3. The third stage of this introductory meditation or introduction to meditation – slowly open your eyes again. Yet as you once again become more aware of the space of this room surrounding your body, stay aware of the inner space or spaces of awareness within your body and of what you are aware of within it. Finally, begin to feel the outer space around your body and the inner spaces within it as non-different or non-dual – as one singular space of pure awareness that extends from an infinite inwardness within your body to the outermost boundaries of the cosmos. Feel this singular space of awareness pervading and vitalising the spaces within every atom and cell of your body.

If, having studied and practiced these stages of meditation, you may find some of the questions below helpful in reviewing your experience of it:

- What sort of things did you become aware of in the space of this room? How did it feel to sense and identify with the space itself and feel it as a field of awareness?

- What sort of things did you become aware of in the felt hollows of your body? How did it feel to give discomforting things more awareness and then identify more with the spaces of awareness in which you felt them?

- What was it like to open your eyes again, be aware of the space around you and yet stay aware of the inner spaces of your body and what you were aware of there?

- What was it like to feel the spaces around and within as one singular, non-dual and unbounded space of pure awareness?

With the new understandings of yoga and meditation presented so far in this essay, let us now return to the question of their relation to counselling. As counsellors or therapists we want our clients to feel safe enough with us to 'open up' – to share things they are aware of. Yet if, like most people, they experience their awareness as a space closed off and bounded by their own bodies – or even just enclosed in their own heads – then surely the first step in counselling and therapy is to help them to open up and expand that very space. For only in this way can they feel it as a space safe enough to share from – which means big enough to easily embrace all that they experience and go through, and with room left over, room big enough to let in other people, to let in new insights and a whole new sense of self.

As counsellors or therapists we also seek to create in our consulting rooms a 'safe space' – a so-called 'holding space' in which people can freely and honestly share their feelings. But if both counsellor and client experience their awareness as something enclosed by their bodies, neither the smallest nor the biggest counselling or therapy room in the world can be actually felt as a safely holding space of awareness – one in which both client and counsellor can feel 'held', and in which both can come to fully let in and embrace each other.

For an awareness-based or yogic counsellor – a practitioner of awareness or 'yogin' – it just needs a single glance at a person's body to see how physically closed or open, enclosed or 'wrapped up' their consciousness is in themselves – how aware or unaware they are of the field or space of awareness around their bodies and the things and people in it, and how narrow or spacious the 'inner space' of awareness is that they can sense and hold open within their bodies.

That is because yoga is not just about the twin realms of mental and emotional experiencing that counselling and psychotherapy focus on. Instead it recognises a *third realm* – that of the senses and of immediate *sensory* experiencing – as more inclusive and fundamental.

Only by cultivating a direct *sensory* experience of emotions in our bodies and a direct sensory experience of mental states in our heads can we stop our thoughts and emotions just feeding off and reinforcing one another in vicious circles. Yet it is surprising how difficult people can find it to get their heads around the thought that *thoughts themselves* can by directly sensed in awareness – for example as mental images, by hearing them as mental words or speech in our minds, or by sensing in our bodies the way they affect our emotions – just as emotions can be directly felt as bodily sensations. To be truly aware of our mental-emotional or somatic states rather than getting wrapped up in them, the first step must be to attend to the qualities belonging to our immediate *sensory* experience of them.

The fact that certain clients may be less willing or find it less satisfactory than others to talk 'about' their mental-emotional states (not least those suffering acute stress or showing signs of so-called borderline and psychotic states) has a good reason. My belief is that for such clients (indeed for all clients if not for all people) what they unknowingly want most of all from another is someone who – like a mother – will take time to first of all give full sensory awareness to their *body*. For only in this way can they feel that their own wordless, bodily sense *of* 'how they are feeling' is being sensed and felt by another – rather than forced into words. For the language, by its very nature, distances our awareness from our immediate sensory experience of our own self, body and state of being.

It is only relatively recently that terms such as 'bodily sensing' and 'somatic resonance' have been coined to refer to this type of direct *sensory* 'empathy' for another person's mental and emotional states. The need to which these terms respond is not just a need to be looked at and listened to in an emotionally sensitive or caring way. Still less is it a need to be drawn out into discussions 'about' one's thoughts and feelings. Instead it is the primordial need to feel one's whole body sensed and embraced by another within the space of an all-round, womb-like space of awareness.

It is the sensory awareness given by the counsellor to the *body* of the client and what it shows, and the all-round spatial *embrace* of this awareness, that helps clients to *feel safer* in their bodies and to get closer to their own sensory experience of themselves – rather than distancing themselves from it through words and talk 'about'. It also helps clients to apply The Awareness Principle themselves, to embrace their own sensory experience of themselves – however stressed or distressing – in a safe and expanded space of awareness.

The emphasis on giving awareness primarily to our immediate sensory experiencing is another important difference, derived from the tantric tradition, between yoga and meditation on the one hand, and psychology and counselling on the other.

A further and most fundamental difference is that yoga and meditation, unlike psychology and counselling, are not merely 'person-centred' – focussed on the personal or inter-personal dimensions of awareness and experience.

For a basic precept of The Awareness Principle is the recognition of the fundamentally *non-individual* or *trans-personal* nature of the awareness within which all personal and inter-personal experiencing occurs. For though people speak casually of 'self-awareness' in connection with 'counselling' and of personal or spiritual 'growth', the deeper truth is that awareness of self cannot – *in principle* – be the private property of any person or self we are *aware of*.

Awareness, in other words, is not essentially 'yours' or 'mine', 'his' or 'hers'. On the contrary, every person's individual sense of 'me-ness' or 'self' is an individualised expression and embodiment of a non-individuated and trans-personal awareness – that ultimate and universal awareness that Indian thought identifies with the Divine, with 'God' or 'God-consciousness'.

One important reason why Indian philosophy is ignored in Western psychology is that it challenges the privatisation of the psyche in Western culture – the reduction of awareness to the private property of persons or a mere biological function of their bodies and brains. As a result, psychological problems suffered by individuals are also privatised – seen as 'their' problem rather than as an expression of a culture which denies any higher, trans-personal or divine dimensions to awareness. In this culture people are *indoctrinated* into believing that consciousness is something bounded by their bodies and a product of their brains. Psychiatry is the pseudo-science founded on this crude biologistic doctrine – which serves nothing but the profits of the pharmaceutical corporations –

and replaces meditation with damagingly awareness-numbing *medication*. The idea that this shallowest of modern doctrines is truer or more 'scientific' than the profound metaphysical understandings of the soul articulated and preserved in Eastern yogic philosophies and practices for millennia is arrogant to say the least.

All the more pity then, that what passes as 'yoga' in the West today has become a mere crass commercialisation and commodification of bodily stretching exercises that have nothing to do with awareness at all, let alone with 'non-dual' awareness.

Taking the word 'yoga' in its root meaning of 'union' – to 'yoke' or 'conjoin' – we can now understand it as a practice of awareness designed to unite our everyday self, the 'experienced self', with another Self, the 'experiencing self'. This experiencing self is nothing but the Awareness Self, that Self which does not 'have' or 'possess' awareness but *is* awareness – an awareness inseparable from that unbounded, absolute, ultimate and universal awareness that Indian thought recognised as the essence of the Divine.

Such metaphysical and spiritual dimensions of awareness cannot be confined to the realm of Eastern spiritual philosophies and traditions however. For they are profoundly relevant to both everyday life and to the theory and practice of counselling. This is because they offer answers to basic questions concerning the essential nature of the self. Yet both the answers and the questions are of a sort which Western psychology and psychiatry continue to ignore, deny or marginalise – blinded as they are by the delusion that awareness is the private property of persons, bounded by the body and a product of the brain. As a result, an individual's mental, emotional or behavioural 'symptoms' are seen merely as diagnostic signs of different categories of 'mental illness' – rather than as *invitations and opportunities* for the sufferer to give themselves more *awareness*.

One final remark is necessary in this context. The Buddhist term 'mindfulness' has now been co-opted into the language of Western psychology and counselling, both in the form of 'Mindfulness Based Cognitive Therapy' and as part of what is called 'Dialectical Behaviour Therapy'. The term 'mindfulness' however (actually a mis-translation of the Sanskrit word for 'memory') is a wholly *imprecise and inappropriate substitute* for the word 'awareness', implying as it does that the 'mind' can in some way be aware of or monitor itself, and that awareness itself is a mere mental state or some form of mental activity. It is not. For whilst pure awareness *embraces* all mental states and activities, it is not itself a mental state or activity – or indeed any activity at all – let alone a function of 'mind' (Sanskrit *Buddhi*). It is awareness and not 'mind' or 'mindfulness' that is the key to the relation between Counselling, Meditation and Yoga.

The Awareness Principle
and Western 'Psychology'

The Awareness Principle is an important basic principle of psychology, yet one that is ignored in contemporary Western understandings of 'consciousness', as well as in 'counselling' and 'psychotherapy' as they have developed in the West. That is because Western psychology has not yet even recognised, as Eastern philosophy has long done, a most basic axiom of the principle itself, namely that awareness as such is quite distinct from its psychological contents, that as 'pure consciousness' it transcends everything we are conscious or aware of. In contrast to the principles of different forms of Western psychology, psychotherapy and psychological counselling, including so-called 'cognitive' therapies, The Awareness Principle does not focus on specific *contents* of consciousness (thoughts, emotions, life event etc.) but rests on a Primary Distinction between all such contents – all elements of our experience – and the larger space or 'field' of awareness in which they arise. Recognising this Primary Distinction allows us to make a Primary Choice – between focussing on, identifying with and thus binding ourselves to the contents of our consciousness – or identifying with the pure awareness of them, an awareness that is innately free of thought, emotional charge or any element of our experience.

The Awareness Principle recognises the transcendental character of awareness. It also recognises its 'immanent' character – that awareness is also present within each and everything we are aware of. Awareness transcends everything we are aware of – for it is the ultimate source of all that is. Precisely because it is the source of everything however, everything we are aware of is also an awareness in its own right. Every sensation, feeling or thought, every physical or mental symptom is itself an awareness of something beyond itself – for example a situation or something going on in another person.

74

A bodily sensation such as hotness or sweating is not just something we are aware of. It is also our way of sensing something beyond it – for example the heat of the Sun or something we are anxious about. Similarly any feeling is not just something we are aware of. Instead it is a 'pre-reflective' or 'unformulated' awareness of something or someone beyond itself (a relationship, situation or life question for example) just as a thought may be a reflective and formulated awareness of something beyond it. Even a bodily symptom or mental state such as anxiety or depression for example, is not just something we are aware of. Nor is it a life 'problem' in itself. Instead the symptom is itself a bodily awareness of a life problem.

The Awareness Principle and the 'Unconscious'

Most of today's high priests of biological psychiatry are quite unable to step outside the box of today's scientific culture. They regard Freudian thinking and traditional psychoanalysis as 'unscientific' because they are not 'evidence-based' or make use of 'unverifiable constructs' such as *ego, id, libido, the unconscious* etc. In this way however, they expose their *unawareness* of the historical evolution of their *own* most basic concepts – failing to recognise that these themselves are no less unverifiable constructs and far from 'evidence-based'. Thus even physical-scientific concepts such as 'quanta', 'matter waves', 'dark energy', not to mention its most basic concepts – the concepts of 'matter' and 'energy' as such – are no less 'unverifiable constructs' than what Freud termed 'the unconscious'. As Martin Heidegger remarked, "physics as physics" – as a theoretical framework which defines its own objects – is not itself the object of any possible physical experiment. Similarly there is no possible scientific experiment that could prove the 'verifiability' of the modern-scientific *concept* of 'energy' or show its superiority to earlier concepts, not least earlier historical understandings of the word 'energy' itself – long since forgotten and altered and distorted in the scientific march of 'progress'. The same applies to the diagnostic categories of so-called 'scientific' psychiatry most of which are mere arbitrarily constructed labels for groups of vaguely defined symptoms.

The fact that scientific terms are constructs – labels that no experiment can verify – does not mean that they lack meaning. Freud's concept of the unconscious may be no more verifiable than those of so-called 'hard science' but that does not mean it does not have meaning or point to something real ('pointing to' being the very meaning of the German verb *bedeuten* – 'to mean'). Freud compared consciousness to a torchlight. Yet every act of using that torchlight to single out and focus on something in the larger field of our awareness, risks blinding us to that field. It is comparable to pointing a torch in the dark – reducing our visual awareness field to what the spotlight of the torch happens to be pointed at and focussed on. Freud was well aware however that meaning has not only to do with some particular element or event in everyday or dream experience that is present in the foreground of our awareness – or that we point at, focus on and single out with the torchlight of our consciousness. Instead he was acutely aware of there being a larger historical, social and personal context to all such singled-out elements or events, and of the way in which the deeper meaning of single elements or events has to do with this larger context. Yet instead of distinguishing our torch-like focal awareness from a quite different type of 'holistic' or 'field' awareness, he stuck to an identification of consciousness with focal awareness – his own favourite tool and still the most respectably scientific tool of investigation. He can be compared to a forensic scientist rigorously searching the psyche in the dark with his torch, always aware that there was something *more* to be seen than what the torch was currently illuminating – something that could therefore provide new material for 'analysis' and add new dimensions of meaning of the visible. Thus he was forever pointing the acute analytic torchlight of his own consciousness in new and different directions, in order to provide clues to these additional dimensions of meaning. The problem is that no matter how serious and rigorous his scientific 'searching in the dark' was, he did not believe in the possibility of simply *switching on the light* – thus illuminating the entire room and entire field of awareness within which all things stand out in their immediate interrelatedness. Consequently the Freudian concept of 'the unconscious' maintained connotations of something innately dark, mysterious and potentially threatening, just as its counterpart – the conscious 'ego' – was seen as the holder and controller of the torch of consciousness, albeit an ego fearful of aiming it in particular directions.

Freud's concept of the 'unconscious' arose from his identification of consciousness *as such* with *focal awareness*. The idea of consciousness having a holistic or field character – the concept of *field awareness* – was therefore replaced by the notion of an 'unconscious', comparable to a room permanently in the dark unless its invisible contents emerged in our dreams, thus also enabling the waking ego to turn its analytic torchlight on them. Freud's identification of consciousness with focal awareness however, was no mere personal failing – for it served the purpose of revealing the identification of 'consciousness' in Western culture purely with the ego and ego-awareness. Yet ego awareness is precisely a type of *focal* awareness which, in restricting itself to singling out specific elements of experience *loses* awareness of their overall field or context of emergence – and of other elements in that field – thus making itself 'unaware' or 'unconscious' of them. Yet even from the point of view of physics, what any 'thing' *is* is determined by the larger field or context of its emergence – 'emergence' being the root meaning of the Greek word *physis* from which the modern term 'physics' derives.

Freud's pioneering work was not indeed a 'discovery' of the unconscious – as if it were some 'thing in itself'. Yet by introducing the notion of 'the unconscious' he pointed to a significant connection between ego-centred, focal awareness on the one hand and the 'unconscious' *memory* or *forgetting* that results from lack of field awareness on the other. For if consciousness is nothing more than focal awareness, a mere torchlight capable of illuminating or singling out only one thing or group of things at a time, then it is only natural that when we switch its focus to some other thing, the first thing can easily be forgotten. Lacking a broader field awareness we cannot retain simultaneous awareness of all the elements within it, thus making them appear as 'unconsciously' forgotten elements. And since ego-awareness is like a torchlight used in the dark – without the light switched on – it is only natural that this field-awareness should be felt by the ego, and seen by Freud, as something intrinsically dark or 'unconscious' – something difficult to *fully* bring to light, and tending to conceal repressed elements of the soul or psyche within it. The dark Freudian unconscious then, became a secular equivalent of the religious concept of Hell. Significantly, this is a word sharing roots with the German adjective 'hell' – meaning 'bright'. How then, does the light of awareness come – through a process of forgetting – to take the form of something dim, dark or 'hellish' of which the ego is unaware or 'unconscious'?

In 'The Singularity of Awareness' Michael Kosok describes the process as a four-stage one:

"We all single out a given ... element of interest, playing, learning, testing, ignoring its context and even childishly forgetting it by dismissal, if only for a moment, like a game of 'make believe'. But then the simple act of ignoring too often leads to a state of ignorance where we "forget that we have forgotten", as the psychologist R.D. Laing so astutely observed. We can see in this simple scenario the beginning of three steps in seed form. The first is fragmentation, which makes possible the activity of 'singling' out elements from a background – to highlight them into view for contrast or comparisons. This may not seem like any kind of serious fragmentation, but it lays the foundation for shifting to focal awareness in contrast to holistic awareness."

"It is interesting to note that in a recent study where Western children were compared to Oriental children in their mode of perception of a pond of fish, Western students immediately focussed on the biggest fish, and only later took into consideration some contextual material. The Eastern students, from the very beginning, described the ongoing holistic pattern of fishes, water and other elements as a singular structure, in which the biggest fish were not that outstanding."

"After fragmentation, then comes dissociation, which means that an act of ignoring takes place, and what is now a background … becomes dissociated from what is focussed on as the important foreground and takes on a minimal value. [Memory] may return in a dream state, or it may simply return within direct awareness. But now the third state enters and this is where dissociation becomes hardened. It is where we not only forget but "forget that we have forgotten" and, as a result, a genuine delusion sets in – together with covering illusions … This is where one begins not to be aware directly – face-to-face – but through a glass darkly."

The 'darkness' lies in perceiving a world of separated or singled out elements or structured complexes of such elements – yet without any sense of the singular unifying light that first brings them to light and embraces them all. This, in terms of many religious philosophies is the 'divine light'. It is understood both in tantric metaphysics and in terms of The Awareness Principle as the very light *of* awareness itself, a light without which 'no-thing' – including light itself – could appear or 'come to light' within awareness.

"Remember what the true 'glasses of divine light' see: each distinction and *particular* form, term or being is fully distinct and unique throughout the entire field of presence, without conflict. However it requires the appropriate centre of vision (the 'eye that is single') to see and experience this Sacred universe of light and love as a truly awesome universe beyond captivity, expressing ranges from the deepest states of tenderness to the highest states of ecstasy. The 'eye that is single' is the *depth* of awareness that goes beyond the dim awareness that is glued to the shallow surface of existence in which all that happens is defined through opposition."

The Awareness Principle is the simple recognition that awareness cannot – in principle – be reduced to a property or function of any thing, being or self that we are aware of. Freud saw 'the unconscious' as the private property of the individual psyche. Jung sensed something wrong here, and thus introduced the notion of a 'collective unconscious'. Neither recognised the essential 'mistake' at stake here, one long recognised in Indian philosophy, namely the basic veiling delusion (*Anavamala*) that awareness can in any way be seen as private property – whether of the individual or 'collective' psyche. There is no more any such thing as 'my' unconscious, 'yours' or 'ours' than there is any such thing as 'my' awareness, 'yours' or 'ours'. On the contrary, awareness itself and as such is that singular reality which both manifests itself in infinite individual and collective forms. It is awareness that individualises or 'individuates' itself, just as it is awareness that collectivises itself in the form of shared cultural identities and 'archetypes'. Awareness is also that 'eye that is single' – the 'third eye'. In practice, Freud – perhaps even more than Jung – was aware of what he himself could only explain as a type of direct 'telepathic' communication between the unconscious of the patient and that of the psychoanalyst. Yet the very question concerning the scientific verifiability of 'telepathy' begs the question. For the question is already based on a pre-conception that awareness or subjectivity, whether in the form of 'consciousness', the 'preconscious' or 'subconscious', or 'the unconscious', is the private property of localised individual subjects, bounded by the individual psyche or their physical body. In contrast, The Awareness Principle recognises the non-local or field character of awareness, and thus also its *innate* function as a communicative medium.

By its very nature, the nature of our silent feeling awareness of ourselves and of others – whether spoken or unspoken – automatically communicates *to* others, whether or not they shine the torchlight of their ego-awareness on it and are therefore 'conscious' of it. Since as beings we are not separate in the first place, but instead inseparable, individual expressions of a singular field of awareness, there is no need of any mechanism of telepathic transmission between individuals to explain the innate inner communication of awareness that occurs between individuals. Being the very medium *out of which* our most private sense of ourselves and others first arises, awareness is also the medium through which it constantly communicates.

The so-called 'conscious' mind is not more but *less* conscious – less aware – than this 'unconscious'. The mystery of 'the unconscious' can thus never be unraveled unless we understand its depths not as depths of 'unawareness' but of *awareness* – not the narrow *focal* awareness of the ego, but all that remains unaware or 'unconscious' for the ego through this narrowness of focus – 'narrowness' (German *Enge*) being, interestingly, both the root meaning of the word anxiety (German *Angst*) and its real-life foundation. It is the ego that 'keeps itself in the dark' and therefore 'anxious' – never switching on the light of field awareness but instead constantly pursuing its own ever-more detailed probings and 'analyses', whether personal or scientific, of what its torchlight focuses on in the dark.

In contrast, 'enlightenment' means 'turning on' the light of awareness. Doing so, we experience the 'unconscious' not as something dim or murky but *as* a larger field of illumination – a *superconsciousness* transcending the narrow ego boundaries of ordinary consciousness. Along with the experience of this 'superconsciousness' goes the experience of a *superself*. This is not a Freudian-style 'superego' made up of internalized social mores or parental judgements. Indeed it is not any self we can be aware *of*. Instead it is that eternal self or 'I' – and that single 'eye' – that does not 'have' or 'possesses' but *is* awareness. This eternal, universal and divine self, the 'Atman' in Indian terms, is one we can come to know only by *being* it – by 'being awareness'. It was named in the very first of the 'Shiva Sutras' – the scriptural aphorism or 'threads' (Sutra) that form the revelatory foundation of the tantric metaphysics and psychology of Kashmir Shaivism. For the Sutra reads simply – 'Chaitanya-atman' – which can be translated as 'Awareness-Being-Self' or 'Awareness *is* the Self'. It is our *unconsciousness of this truth* – the truth that awareness is not only the essence of 'the unconscious' but also the essence of 'self' – that is the basis of all theories of 'the unconscious' and the key to their deeper significance.

The flip side of 'un-consciousness' is a sustained awareness of the 'un-', of all that ordinary normal consciousness, with its narrowed focus, tends to consistently ignore, forget and in turn forget that it has forgotten, identifying its own truly 'unconscious' state of *unawareness* as 'ordinary' or 'normal' consciousness – and even taking this ordinary consciousness as a benchmark both of mental health and 'scientific' knowledge. This is the basic error that Freud challenged, unlike today's haughty scientists and psychiatrists who remain stuck in it. Since his time however, the latter have persisted in their search for a material or biological or evolutionary basis for 'consciousness', whilst never pausing to consider the basic paradox – made explicit through The Awareness Principle – namely that since it is a singular *field* of subjectivity and not some subject or object within that field, awareness cannot be explained by any thing or collection of things that we single out and focus on within that field – including the human brain and its 'hard-wiring'. The aim of articulating The Awareness Principle will be fulfilled even if all it does is to show how so-called 'hard' science' has, in reality, the weakest and least solid of philosophical foundations, thus undermining its attacks, not only on Freud and psychoanalysis, but on a whole range of alternative scientific and spiritual world views with a far longer tradition and far firmer foundations – albeit long forgotten ones.

Aphorisms on Awareness

Awareness *is* the Self.

Thus identifying individual awareness with universal awareness and attaining divine bliss, from where or from whom should one get scared?

The Shiva Sutras of Vasugupta

Every appearance owes its existence to the light of awareness. Nothing can have its own being without the light of awareness.

Kshemaraja

Meditate on one's own body as the universe,
and as having the nature of awareness.

The yogi is always mindful of that witnessing awareness
which alone is the subject of everything,
which is always a subject and never an object.

The Vijnanabhairava Tantra

Having made itself manifest, awareness abides as both
the inner and the outer.

Utpaladeva

The being of all things that are recognised in awareness
in turn depends on awareness.

Abhinavagupta

Awareness is devoid of objects;
That is why it is called
Eternally free from bonds.

Mandukya Karika

The body *is* an awareness.

For seers, to be alive means to be aware.

There is something in us all that can witness with our entire body.

Carlos Castaneda

"… awareness qua awareness [is] not awareness as a topic within, or relative to, *a context that defines it by confining* it, as e.g. social awareness, physical awareness or awareness physically analysed … Rather, without trepidation, awareness 'itself' – awareness without confinement – is our topic; awareness without imposed limits as our 'context'… Awareness as such is a truly primitive term, unlike 'consciousness' (with all its differentiated levels) which … always refers to being 'aware-of-something', of some content, as vivid or vague, sharp or dim as it may be. Awareness … belongs to no one exclusively, has no restrictions, derivations or explanations … *just is*. Awareness is a singularity beyond personality and impersonality – which cannot be contained, curtailed, expanded or transcended from 'without awareness'. It is not as important to simply label this awareness with a word like God, the Absolute or what have you, as to *submit* and *abandon* yourself to this singularity of awareness … the awareness that runs *through* you as one person *of* a multi-personal universe of unlimited awareness …

[This] 'spiritual' awareness cannot be locked up in churches, temples and mosques ... from which imposing directives issue forth, nor can it thrive diluted as part of the mainstream culture it is supposed to be educating."

Awareness 'itself' is going nowhere, is doing nothing 'outside' of itself, there not being anything outside: it belongs to no one exclusively, has no restrictions, derivations or explanations ... awareness *just* is.

Awareness is a singularity beyond personality and impersonality – which cannot be contained, curtailed, expanded or transcended from 'without awareness'.

It is not important to simply label this awareness with a word like God, the Absolute or what have you, as to *submit* and *abandon* yourself to this singularity of awareness ...the awareness that runs *through* you as one person *of* an multi-personal universe of unlimited awareness ...

Spiritual awareness cannot be locked up in churches, temples and mosques ... from which imposing directives issue forth, nor can it thrive diluted as part of the mainstream culture it is supposed to be educating ..."

Michael Kosok – 'The Singularity of Awareness'

"Now thinking which constructs a world of objects understands these objects; but meditative thinking begins with an awareness of the field within which these objects are ... the field of awareness itself."

John Anderson – from his introduction to
Martin Heidegger's 'Discourse on Thinking'

The most fundamental scientific 'fact' of all is not the existence of a universe of things in space and time but an *awareness* of such a universe. We can no more explain awareness *as such* by any 'thing' we are *aware of* than we can explain *dreaming* as such by something we *dream of.* Awareness is nothing in need of scientific 'explanation'. For by its very nature it is 'no-thing', and thus not explainable by some other things. Awareness is nothing explainable by or enclosed within our bodies or brains. It is the very *space* within which we experience all things – including our bodies themselves.

Awareness is everything.

Everything is an awareness.

Peter Wilberg

Part 4

Awareness Based Cognitive Therapy

...as simple as ABC

Contents

Introduction

What is Awareness Based Cognitive Therapy?

Awareness-Based Cognitive Therapy (ABCT) is a new form of 'Non-Dual' counselling and therapy – meaning that it is derived from insights rooted in Indian yogic philosophy and practice.

The original and concise distillation of these insights is termed **The Awareness Principle**. This principle also finds expression in the manifold **Practices of Awareness** which together constitute what I call 'The New Yoga of Awareness'. In contrast to other forms of therapy including other 'cognitive' therapies, its focus does not lie on the specific contents of consciousness (events, thoughts, feelings etc) or their relation, but rather on a Primary Distinction between *all* such contents – all elements of our experience – and the larger space or 'field' of awareness in which they arise.

Who can benefit from ABCT?

Counsellors and psychotherapists, physicians, psychiatrist and other health professionals, alternative health practitioners, life coaches, teachers and social workers and carers – and all those seeking help or counselling from them.

How can they benefit?

1. By learning to be fully aware of and open to their own subjective experience and emotions and those of individuals in their care, but …

   o **Without** being overwhelmed by them.

   o **Without** feeling them as a source of constant 'stress'.

o **Without** having to shut out or act out, suppress or somatise their experience.

o **Without** having to hide themselves behind a professional mask, role or persona.

o **Without** having to clinically objectify or label another person's distress or dis-ease.

o **Instead** being open to and able to respond to any experience, person or situation in an aware, free and non-reactive way.

2. By showing those seeking their aid or care how they also can be fully aware of and open to their own subjective experience of themselves and others, but …

o **Without** being overwhelmed by their experience.

o **Without** thinking there is something 'wrong' with them.

o **Without** identifying with their experience and reacting from it.

o **Without** needing to label their feelings with catchwords such us as 'stress', 'anxiety' or 'depression'.

o **Without** having to shut out or 'act out', suppress or 'somatise' their experience.

o **Without** having to identify their felt 'dis-ease' with a labelled medical or psychiatric 'disease' or 'disorder'.

o **Without** having to identify with medical labels and/or with the roles of bad, mad, sick or 'difficult' people.

Who You Are

Who are you?

You are not what you think.

You are not the self you experience.

You are not your experience of yourself.

You are not your experience of the world.

You are more than the sum of all your experiences.

You are more than the sum of all you have ever experienced.

You are the awareness of all you experience within and around you.

That awareness is the true experiencer of all you experience.

That awareness is not bounded by your body or mind.

That awareness is not the property of any self or 'I'.

Still less is it a product of your mind or body.

Instead you, your body and your mind, are

Shapes taken by awareness,

Within awareness.

The Primary Distinction

There is the way we are feeling.
There is the way we think about it.
There is the way we express our thoughts and feelings.
There is the way they colour our view of the world.
There is the way they influence how we see others.
There is the way they shape our sense of ourselves.
There is the way they lead us to behave.
There is the way they affect our bodies.

And there is **AWARENESS** …

Awareness of our thoughts and feelings.
Awareness of the way we express them.
Awareness of the way they affect our bodies and behaviour.
Awareness of how they lead us to act and react to others.
Awareness of the way they colour our view of the world.
Awareness of the way they affect our sense of ourselves.

And yet…

This awareness of our feelings and thoughts is not itself a feeling or thought.
This awareness of our bodies and minds is not itself anything bodily or mental.
This awareness embraces and also transcends each and every thing we are aware of.
That is why it has been called 'universal' and 'transcendental'.

Identifying with this 'transcendental' awareness transforms us. It frees us from identification with our bodies and minds, with our feelings and thoughts, sensations and perceptions, actions and reactions, behaviours and beliefs. At the same time it creates space for new, clearer feelings and thoughts to arise – and with them a new sense of ourselves. A sense of that Self that is not simply aware of this, that or the other. A self that is not simply aware but rather IS awareness – pure and simple. Not 'my' or 'your' awareness, but an awareness transcending 'I' and 'You'. The self that is nothing but pure awareness – the 'Awareness Self' – was known in the Indian philosophical tradition of 'Non-Duality' or 'Advaita' as the *Atman* or *Chaitanyatman*. Achieving identity with this Self is the aim of all 'Non-Dual' or Advaitic traditions.

The Awareness Principle

The Awareness Principle is an important basic principle of psychology, yet one that is ignored in contemporary Western understandings of 'consciousness', as well as in 'counselling' and 'psychotherapy' as they have developed in the West.

That is because Western psychology has not yet recognised, as Eastern philosophy has long done, a most basic axiom of the principle itself, namely that awareness as such is quite distinct from its psychological contents, that as 'pure consciousness' it transcends everything we are conscious or aware *of.*

The Awareness Principle recognises the 'transcendental' character of awareness. It also recognises its 'immanent' character – that awareness is also present *within* each and everything we are aware of. Awareness transcends everything we are aware of – for it is the ultimate source of all that is. Precisely because it is the source of everything however, everything we are aware of also *is* an awareness in its own right.

Every sensation, feeling or thought, every physical or mental symptom – indeed every part of our body and mind – is itself an awareness of something *beyond itself* – for example a situation or something going on in another person.

A bodily sensation such as hotness or sweating is not just something we are aware of. It is also our way of sensing something beyond it – for example the heat of the Sun or something we are anxious about. Similarly any feeling is not just something we are aware of. Instead it is a 'pre-reflective' or 'unformulated' awareness of something or someone beyond itself (a relationship, situation or life question for example) just as a thought may be a reflective and formulated awareness of something beyond it. And a bodily symptom or mental state such as anxiety or depression for example, is not just something we are *aware of.* Nor is it a life 'problem' in itself. Instead the symptom is itself a bodily *awareness* of a life problem.

The Awareness Principle unites two major precepts therefore:

1. Awareness *is everything*

2. Everything *is an awareness.*

The two precepts are united by an understanding that since every atom and molecule, cell and organ, being or body, person or planet, is a shape taken by a universal awareness that is its source. In Awareness Based Cognitive Therapy these two aspects of The Awareness Principle are united by a three-stage Practice of Awareness:

1. Giving time to be *aware* of each and every element of our experience, in an immediate, sensual bodily way – and *affirming*

them all, whether or not they are experienced as 'positive' or 'negative'.

2. Ceasing to *identify* with any elements of our experience as such, but instead identifying and expanding with the spaces of pure awareness, inner and outer, *within* which we experience them – and affirming them from and within that awareness.

3. Coming to a recognition of the different life-questions or aspects of our life-world and relationships that each and every element of our lived experience is itself *an awareness of*.

The Awareness Principle and Therapy

There are many new 'approaches' to medicine, counselling, mental health and psychotherapy. The Awareness Principle on the other hand, as its name implies, is not simply a new 'approach' but a fundamentally new therapeutic principle or 'paradigm'. As well as being a new therapeutic principle however, The Awareness Principle is also a fundamentally new philosophical principle, one that in turn provides the foundation of a new scientific principle or 'paradigm', a new medical principle, a new psychological and sociological principle, a new meditational principle – and a new spiritual and religious principle. Above all, The Awareness Principle is a new and highly practical life principle – a principle to live by.

Out of The Awareness Principle comes an entire range of new Practices or 'Yogas' of awareness. These Practices of Awareness provide a new foundation for life, just as it is The Awareness Principle itself that provides a new foundation for science. The Awareness Principle is the guiding principle for The Practice of Awareness. It is through Practicing Awareness in life that the Awareness Principle itself truly comes to life – not just as an abstract principle but as a way of life, not just as a philosophical or scientific principle, but as an intrinsically therapeutic life-principle.

The Awareness Principle as such is neither old nor new but is an 'old-new' principle. Its groundbreaking and authentic originality or 'newness' comes from making fully explicit – for the first time and in an entirely new way – a primary truth or 'first principle' recognised long ago. And whilst this first principle is implicit in both life and science – as well as in many forms of counselling, meditation and psychotherapy – its primary truth is still unrecognised. As a result, it has remained unformulated as a primary principle or 'first principle' – as a principle of both life and science. As a first principle it has been replaced by the principle of 'first causes' – whether of life and the universe as a whole, health and ill-health, or of human experience in all its shapes.

Whenever a new therapeutic principle or practice is announced, the key questions asked about it in today's economically governed world are:

- whether it is effective?
- whether it is economic?
- whether it is 'evidence-based' and therefore 'scientific'?

The final question is the most fundamental one in relation to the first two, for it rests on an unquestioned concept of 'science' itself. This concept in turn has lead to counter-productive notions of 'effectiveness' and 'economy' based solely on so-called 'objective' criteria – those that can be reduced to measurable quantities. The basic presuppositions of the dominant Western conception of 'science' are not themselves the object of any possible scientific experiment. The Awareness Principle is a new *scientific* as well as therapeutic principle because it challenges these presuppositions in the most evidential or empirical way possible – in a way more 'scientific' than 'science' itself. It does so by recognising that the first, most self-evidential, experiential, 'empirical' or 'scientific' fact is NOT the 'objective' existence of a universe of things but *subjective awareness* of that universe. That awareness however, is not itself any sort of 'thing' or 'object' – and therefore cannot, in principle, be explained by or reduced to any thing or things we are aware of. The most basic presupposition of science is that it identifies reality with *objectivity*. The Awareness Principle reasserts the primary, universal reality of *subjectivity* – of awareness.

Basic Axioms of The Awareness Principle

1.   The central axiom or 'First Principle' of 'The Awareness Principle' is that Awareness itself – and not any thing or universe of things we are aware *of* – is the First Principle of the universe.

2.   Awareness is the 'transcendental' condition – the 'pre-condition' or 'field condition' – for our awareness of any thing or universe of things whatsoever.

3.   Awareness embraces and transcends all that we experience or are aware *of* – all 'contents' of consciousness and all elements of our experience.

4.   Just as dreaming cannot be explained by or reduced to anything we *dream of*, nor can awareness be explained by or reduced to any thing or things we are *aware of* (for example matter or energy, the body or brain).

5.   Just as space is inseparable but at the same time quite distinct from every object in it, so is awareness inseparable and at the same time quite distinct from each and every thing we are aware of.

6.	Just as space embraces, permeates and transcends every object in it, so does awareness embrace, permeate and transcend everything we are aware of in it.

7.	Awareness of things is not itself a thing. Thus awareness of a localised object in space is not itself a localised object in space – it is non-local and object-free.

8.	Awareness of a bodily sensation or symptom, drive or impulse, action or behaviourial pattern, emotion or thought *is not itself* a sensation or symptom, drive or impulse, action or behavioural pattern, and is therefore intrinsically *free* of all such contents of consciousness.

9.	Everything we are aware of also *is* an awareness. A feeling is an awareness of something – and not just something we are aware of, and so is a bodily sensation or symptom. Awareness is therefore not only 'transcendent' but also 'immanent' – present *within* all things.

Basic Maxims of
The Awareness Principle

The awareness of any content of consciousness is not itself a content of consciousness. It is essentially content-free.

The awareness of any thing – is not itself a thing. It is thing-free.

The awareness of a thought is not itself a thought. It is thought-free.

The awareness of a feeling is not itself a feeling. It is feeling-free.

The awareness of a sensation is not itself a sensation.
It is free of sensation.

The awareness of an urge or impulse to act or react does not itself impel us to react. It is action and reaction-free.

From Focal to Field Awareness

Most forms of counselling and psychotherapy – including traditional forms of Cognitive Therapy – take as their starting point particular elements of our experience or 'contents' of consciousness – whether life situations or events, 'dysfunctional' thoughts, emotions or body sensations, dream symbols or somatic symptoms, reactive or 'maladaptive' behaviours. They then seek to link these, intuitively or 'scientifically' in chains of 'causes' and 'effects' (Diagram 1). Even if multiple causal 'factors' or reciprocal relationships between different elements are admitted, the model remains based only on *linear* relations between elements. Other models (Diagram 2) see the different elements of our experience as part of a structured whole, a 'complex' or 'gestalt' that is more than the sum of its parts.

Diagram 1   **Diagram 2**

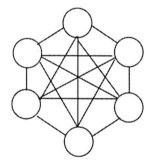

Both models reduce the individual soul or psyche to separable elements of the individual's experience, whether linked in causal chains or seen as structures or 'complexes' of interrelated elements. They ignore the larger background field of *awareness* (hatched area in Diagram 3) from and within which *all* elements of our experience emerge.

Diagram 3

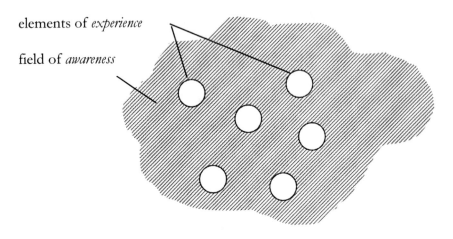

elements of *experience*

field of *awareness*

The more bounded and contracted our awareness field becomes however (see bounded area in Diagram 4) the less elements of our experience we are aware of within it.

Diagram 4

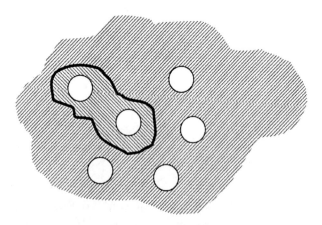

If we identify with the spacious *field* dimension of awareness on the other hand, we not only embrace more elements of our actual experience in awareness, but also create space to allow hitherto hidden or latent elements of our experience (grey-shaded circles in Diagram 5) to emerge into awareness.

Diagram 5

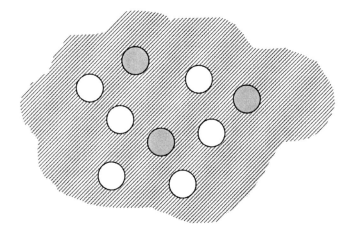

Awareness Based Cognitive Therapy is about maintaining a defocussed field awareness rather than merely seeking to focus on and objectify particular contents of consciousness or elements of our experience within our awareness field.

In contrast to field awareness, focal awareness assumes some sort of fixed centre or 'locus' of consciousness from which we focus on and objectify different elements of our experience within it. In reality, there is no central locus or 'subject' of consciousness from which we can focus on and *objectify* our experience that is not itself a subjective element *of* our experience. Thus even thoughts or feelings *about* different elements of our experience are a *part* of our experience – and therefore nothing separate or apart from the common *field* of awareness from which all such elements of experience or contents of consciousness emerge.

Awareness Based Cognitive Therapy

The more we *focus* awareness on any given element(s) of our experience however, the less sense we have of the larger background *field* of awareness within which alone they arise, and come to stand out or 'ex-ist'. This spacious and expansive *awareness field* is both distinct but inseparable from all the elements of experience of conents of conscious that arise as expressions of it. That is why **Awareness Based Cognitive Therapy** is based on a 'Primary Distinction' – the distinction between all such contents of consciousness and elements of experience – every possible thing we are aware of – and *awareness as such*. Instead of encouraging the client to focus awareness on *localised contents* of consciousness or *elements of experience* such as bodily sensations, thoughts, recollections or emotions and to turn these into clinical 'objects' of analysis and manipulation, the aim of **ABCT** is to help the client to experience the essentially non-local or 'field' character of awareness – and the inherent freeing and therapeutic effect of identifying with this 'meta-cognitive', 'transcendental' or *field awareness*.

The aims of **ABCT** are achieved on the basis of the following 'four recognitions':

1. Recognition of **The Primary Distinction** – between awareness as such and specific things we are aware of (contents of consciousness).
2. Recognition that awareness, like space, *transcends* all we perceive or experience within it.
3. Recognition of **The Primary Choice** – between identifying with things we experience, or identifying with the spacious *awareness field* in which we experience them.
4. Recognition that awareness is not only 'transcendent' but 'immanent' – present within all things, and that therefore anything we are aware of, including thoughts, emotions, sensations or symptoms of dis-ease, is *itself* an awareness.

These four recognitions allow the client to practice what can be termed **The Primary Awareness Cycle**:

1. **Being Aware** of all there is to be aware of. This needs time. Giving ourselves the necessary time to be more aware and aware of more is the common essence of both therapy and meditation.

2. **Bodying Awareness** – not verbally labelling the things we are aware of but giving ourselves time to be aware of our bodies and of our wordless bodily awareness of things.

3. **Being Awareness** – giving ourselves time to distinguish anything we are aware of from the very awareness of it – and identifying with or 'being' that awareness itself.

4. **Being the Awareness that things themselves are** – giving ourselves time to feel what any 'thing' we are aware of (for example a mood, body sensation or symptom) is itself a (hidden or indirect) awareness of. In this way we no longer experience the thing as a thing or mental 'object of consciousness' at all but as a consciousness in its own right – awareness of something or someone else beyond it – thus returning us to step 1 in the awareness cycle (**Being Aware**).

Basic Awareness-Raising Questions

1. Name one thing you are aware of in the space around you.
2. Example answer: 'a notepad'.

1. Name one or more *sensory* qualities of that thing you are aware of.
2. Example answer: 'white' and 'made of paper'.

1. Can you distinguish between the thing and the space around it? (Yes)
2. Could you be aware of the thing without a space in which to be aware of it? (No)

1. Is the space in which you are aware of the thing 'white' or 'made of 'paper'? (No)
2. Is the awareness of the thing 'white' or 'made of paper? (No)

1. Name one thing you are aware of inside you
   Example answer: 'depression'.
2. Name one or more *sensory* quality of that 'depression'
   Example answer: feeling 'heavy' or 'pulled down' into myself.
3. Name one thing that that 'depression' is itself an awareness of.

1. Can you let yourself sense and identify with the spaces in which you are aware of both thoughts and things, instead of with those thoughts and things themselves?
2. Can you distinguish between thoughts you are aware of in your head and the inner head space in which you are aware of them? (Yes)

The 'ABC' of ABCT

'A' for Awareness and Action

The aim of ABCT is to cultivate an on-going Awareness of all the different dimensions of our experience within the moment, and at the same time distinguish that awareness from any specific thing we experience or are aware of – including our overall self-experience. Being distinct from anything we are aware of, awareness is what frees us from passive identification with different elements of our mental, emotional and bodily experience. In this way it also allows us to act in ways that are not simply a reaction to our experience of ourselves, other people and the world.

'B' for Bodyhood and Breathing

The term 'mindfulness' is a poor and misleading substitute for 'awareness'. That is because awareness is not a product of 'the mind' or something purely mental. Awareness itself is neither mental nor bodily. It is awareness <u>of</u> our bodies and minds, our bodies *as well* as our minds. Only through awareness of body and mind – not just mental awareness – can we become more aware of the interaction between the direct wordless, bodily dimensions of our experiencing and their mental reflection in thought and language. That is why the cultivation of sustained awareness is impossible without full body awareness – 'bodyfulness' as well as 'mindfulness'. We breathe air through our mouths and noses into our lungs but it is with and through our entire body surface – and all our body's senses – that we breathe in our awareness of ourselves, other people and the world. Awareness of our breathing is the key to awareness of our body and self as a whole. ABCT is about giving ourselves breathing space –

time and space in which to simply be aware. Awareness itself is not a product or property of the body or brain, nor bounded by them. It is awareness itself that 'bodies' – taking on countless bodily shapes and communicating through the language of the body as well as through the word.

'C' for Communication and Cognition

We do not need to verbally share all the things of which we are silently 'cognisant' or aware. For that silent awareness of ourselves and others communicates directly <u>to</u> others whether or not we express it in words. Yet both everyday inter-personal communication and counselling or therapeutic communication ('talking cures') are distorted by the belief that verbal 'sharing' is essential for the awakening and communication of awareness. It is the other way round. Only through the direct cultivation of mental, emotional and bodily awareness can we communicate that awareness to others directly – not just 'in words' but 'through the word' ('dia-logically') and through the language of the body. Verbally 'sharing' things we are 'cognisant' or aware of – not least in counselling or therapy – easily becomes a substitute for silently deepening the direct awareness of them, and thus communicating, silently or through the word, from this deepened awareness.

'ABCT' and 'CBT'

Traditional forms of 'C.B.T.' – 'Cognitive-Behavioural Therapy' – are now the most highly-promoted form of non-drugs based psychotherapy. Their common and central claim is that it is a "scientific fact" that "our thoughts cause our feelings and behaviours, not external things, like people, situations and events". (National Association of Cognitive Behavioral Therapists). It is absolutely true that our thoughts *about* things affect our emotional reactions <u>to</u> them, and may therefore intensify or reinforce habitual feelings or behaviours towards them. Yet someone whose life has just been affected by such 'things' as losing a job – or a bomb wiping out their entire family – will not easily be convinced of the 'scientific fact' that what they are feeling is 'caused' by their thoughts and not these 'things'. For their 'depression' is not a 'thing in itself' – neither a brain disorder nor a mechanical effect of their thoughts. It is the expression of an *awareness* of undeniable things.

Proponents and practitioners of traditional C.B.T. are certainly right in claiming that people can change the way they feel and act by changing the way they think – in particular so-called 'automatic thoughts' they have in response to situations. The simple fact of the matter however, is that we cannot change a single thought or thing without first being aware of it. A thought itself is just as much a thing we are aware of as any other thing – whether a feeling, event, person or object. Yet this subjective awareness of our thoughts is something quite different from turning them into objects of our mind or intellect – *objects of other thoughts.* The practice of C.B.T. on the other hand, rests on the therapist turning the client's thoughts into clinical objects of the therapist's own 'scientific' thoughts. That is why, although their focus may be on the client's 'automatic thoughts' and their unwanted emotional effects, most 'Cognitive Behavioural Therapists' are unaware of the paradox that their own 'Cognition' of their clients and their Therapeutic Behaviour towards them is shaped by thoughts no less 'automatic' than those of their clients – albeit ones that spring from their supposedly 'scientific' theories. Like traditional CBT, ABCT is essentially a form of 'psycho-education' – specifically 'Education in Awareness'. For in contrast to CBT it recognises that awareness as such – being both thought-free and thing-free – can instantly and automatically free us from identifying emotionally with 'automatic' thoughts about things. And yet we cannot be aware of our thoughts without giving ourselves *Time to Be Aware* – the very essence of both therapy and meditation.

'Awareness Based Cognitive Therapy' could also be termed 'Re-cognitive Behavioural Therapy'. That is because awareness is what allows us to recognise our thoughts about things as just that – thoughts. This prevents us from confusing our thoughts with the very things they are about – for example with the events they might be a response to or the feelings they may seek to give expression to. Recognising thoughts AS thoughts is what prevents us from both identifying with our thoughts and from identifying thoughts about reality with reality. Yet to recognise thoughts AS thoughts means being aware of them as 'things in themselves' – albeit 'thought-things' that we experience in our inner mind space, and not the sort of 'things' we experience in physical space. C.B.T. declares it to be an objective "scientific fact" that it is thoughts, not things, that cause people to feel and act the way they do. In contrast, neither Thoughts <u>nor</u> Things can in any way 'cause' people to act or feel the way they do if they are aware of *both* as distinct things.

The Historic Roots of ABCT

The Awareness Principle and Awareness Based Cognitive Therapy have their roots in the 'Doctrine of Recognition' central to the tantric philosophies of 'Kashmir Shaivism', as expounded by its principal teachers or 'gurus' – Utpaladeva, Somananda, Abhinavagupta, and Kshemaraja. At the heart of the Doctrine of Recognition is the understanding that ultimate reality has the character of an unbounded space or field of awareness that is the source of all things and that comes to recognise itself in each and every thing experienced within it. Like The Awareness Principle, 'The Doctrine of Recognition' recognises all 'experiencing' and all 'cognition' as essentially subjective – NOT as a 'cognition' of 'objects' by isolated 'subjects' or 'selves', but as the self-*recognition* of universal subjectivity or awareness in every thing it experiences.

"things that have fallen to the level of [being seen as] objects of cognition … are [in reality] essentially awareness"

Utpaladeva

We do not cognise our bodies primarily as 'objects', of perception or reflection. Instead we experience them – subjectively – from within. The same principle applies not only to our experience of our own bodies but to our entire experience of the world around us and every 'thing' within it. For these too, are not essentially 'objects' of perception or reflection but an experiential reflection of a transcendental 'witnessing' awareness or subjectivity. Similarly, what we call 'thinking' does not turn things we experience into 'objects' of 'cognition' or mental 'reflection'. Instead thought itself IS the reflection of direct subjective awareness of all we experience. It is through the self-reflection of awareness in both things and thoughts that awareness comes to recognise itself in both.

That is why, as long as we continue to even think of things as mere 'objects' of 'cognition' – whether sensory, emotional or intellectual – we fail to achieve a state of truly awareness-based or 'recognitive' experiencing. For aware experiencing means being able to distinguish each and every thing we experience from the very awareness of experiencing it – the 'Primary Distinction' central to ABCT. The intellectual understanding and recognition of this distinction in thought is itself central to applying it in life. Not only is there is no contradiction whatsoever between use of the thinking intellect and abiding in meditative thought-free awareness. The very terms and concepts of ABCT, rooted in the Basic Axioms and Maxims of 'The Awareness Principle' are themselves recognitions of a word- and thought-free awareness – that awareness which, according to the *Vijnanabhairava Tantra* **"is always a subject and never an object."** As such these axioms and maxims serve as 'mantra' by which to guard ('-tra') that object-free awareness ('man') and to liberate ourselves through it.

ABCT and Mindfulness-Based Cognitive Therapy

Though ABCT shares many important and valuable basic understandings with so-called 'Mindfulness Based Cognitive Therapy' (MBCT), there are also significance differences. MBCT is an eclectic mix of approaches drawn from Buddhism, cognitive therapies, body-oriented psychotherapies and neuroscience. It also uses an eclectic variety of terms such as *meditation, mindfulness, attention, mindful attention, witnessing, being present* and *awareness* in an almost wholly undefined, undifferentiated or synonymous way. ABCT on the other hand, is based on the practice of a single clear principle – 'The Awareness Principle' – and on a *single foundational term* – not 'mindfulness' but *awareness*. In this way it both refines and unifies – conceptually and in practice – all the most central and most valuable insights of MBCT. Another significant difference from ABCT is that MBCT was developed as an approach to treating 'depression'. In doing so it passively adopts the conventional cultural and medical-model view of depression as a pathological state or 'illness'. Thus although MBCT teaches techniques which encourage patients to disengage from negative patterns of mental activity which reinforce and fixate chronic *depressive states*, it fails to recognise the innately healing role of the *depressive process*. This process is nature's own substitute for *meditation* in a manic business culture of pressurised 'busy-ness' – one which sees feeling 'down' and 'low' or mentally slow or 'ruminative' – *meditative* – as 'negative and, above all, as economically unproductive. The depressive process is thus precisely what such a pressuring culture needs as a healthy balance – helping individuals to slow down, to fully reinhabit their bodies and to relate to the world from a deeper, more inward place within themselves – something much needed in a world in which there are *good reasons* for feeling depressed. True 'mindfulness' is an emergence of clear insight from a deep *bodily awareness* of the *questions* pregnant in all 'negative' feelings. This is quite different from experiencing our minds as preoccupied or 'full' with unhelpfully negative thoughts – the very type of *mind-fulness* that MBCT seeks to overcome – whilst ignoring this very connotation of the word itself – which is anyway a misleading translation of the corresponding Buddhist term. That is why ABCT speaks of *awareness* rather than 'mindfulness', recognising as it does that the *pure awareness* of emotions, thoughts and of 'mind' itself, is, *in principle*, something innately free of emotion and thought – *mind-free* rather than 'mind-full'.

Primary Principles and Practices of Awareness
The Foundations of Awareness Based Cognitive Therapy

The Primary Question – how do we know that anything is or exists at all, including ourselves? The answer – only through *an awareness* of experiencing it.

The Primary Word – not 'Being', 'Love', 'Energy', 'Spirit', 'Soul', 'Body', 'Mind' or 'Mindfulness' but 'Awareness' – for we only *know* of any such thing we might call 'energy', 'being', 'spirit', 'love' etc. through an *awareness* of it.

The Primary Principle – awareness itself IS the 'First Principle' and ultimate foundation of all that is. Like empty space, it both pervades and transcends all things within it.

The Primary Distinction – awareness, like empty space, is *absolutely distinct* from any particular thing we experience within it.

The Primary Sense – sensing our body surface and the entire space around it as a space of pure awareness, and feeling ourselves breathing this clear space or 'air' of awareness through every pore of our skin.

The Primary Choice – to identify with whatever we are experiencing (for example a situation, person, event, thought or emotion) or to identify with the pure *awareness* of experiencing it.

The Primary Means – The primary means of identifying with pure awareness is to sense and identify with the spaces – inner and outer – *within* which we experience things.

The Primary Mantram – whatever you are experiencing do not think to yourself " 'I' am experiencing such and such" but rather "**There is an awareness** of experiencing such and such' or alternatively 'IT – **awareness as such** – is experiencing such and such."

The Primary Recognition – recognising that the *awareness* of any thing or thought, impulse or emotion we experience is *not itself* a thing or thought, impulse or emotion – and therefore is innately *free* of any thing or thought, impulse or emotion.

The Primary Maxims

Awareness of any thing is not itself a thing.
It is innately thing-free.

Awareness of a thought is not itself a thought.
It is innately thought-free.

Awareness of an emotion is not itself a feeling.
It is innately feeling-free.

Awareness of a pain or sensation is not itself a sensation.
It is innately sensation free.

Awareness of mind is not itself anything 'mental'.
It is innately mind-free.

Awareness of our bodies is not itself anything bodily.
It is innately body-free and body-less.

Awareness of self is not the property of any self.

The Primary Self – that self which does not regard itself as 'having' or 'awareness but instead recognises that its essence IS awareness, pure and simple.

The Primary Body – not the 'physical' body as we perceive it from the outside, but the *felt body* – the body as we feel it from inside. This is our body of *feeling awareness* or soul – embracing all we experience, both within and around our 'physical' bodies.

The Primary Practice – to meditate. Meditation here does not mean 'doing' anything but rather taking short intervals of time for 'not doing' after *each and every* daily task, activity or *focus of awareness* – rather than just 'going from one thing to another' throughout the day and only taking time to rest or reflect at the end. In particular it means *taking time to be aware* – coming to rest in a state of *unfocussed awareness* in which we can (a) give ourselves time to sense in our bodies where what have just been doing or focussing on has left us, whilst at the same time (b) become aware of *more* of our bodies, selves, lives, environment and world *as a whole.* In this way we create 'breathing spaces' of awareness in which new insights can come to light from awareness – and during which we can choose what to do or focus on next in an aware way, rather than in an automatic, habitual or robotic way (see **The Primary Freedom**).

The Primary Equations – (1) every mental-emotional state is at the same time a bodily or somatic state, and can be sensed *as such* through the cultivation of heightened bodily awareness (2) we are as much aware of our being or self *as a whole* as we are aware of our *body* as a whole (both upper and lower body) and the space around it.

The Primary Shift – to shift awareness primarily *to* our immediate sensuous and bodily experience of whatever we are aware of experiencing, 'positive' or 'negative' – sensing all mental-emotional states as nothing but different bodily textures, densities and mood-colours or 'tonalities' of awareness.

The Primary Stance – to fully and unreservedly feel and affirm everything we are aware of experiencing – whether 'positive' or 'negative' – whilst at the same time distinguishing every element of our experience from the pure awareness of experiencing it – and *identifying* with that very awareness (see **The Primary Distinction** and **The Primary Choice**).

The Primary Centre – a centre of both awareness and breathing in the lower abdomen, called 'hara' in Japanese. Seating our awareness and breathing in this still and silent 'hara' centre prevents us identifying with our head *or* hearts, mind *or* emotions.

The Primary Exercise – standing or sitting (1) be aware of your head, chest and entire upper body above the waist (2) be aware of the ground beneath your feet, your legs and entire lower body below the waist (3) sense the inner space of your lower abdomen or hara (see **The Primary Centre**) and centre you awareness at a point deep down within it – a few inches below and behind the navel. This is your spiritual and physical centre of gravity.

The Primary Breath Cycle – (1) always *beginning* each in-breath using the abdominal muscles alone, feeling the abdomen pushing put and expanding like a hollow balloon – and in doing so filling with *awareness* (2) as each of exhalation of air comes to an end, allowing an interval before the next in-breath – one in which we feel the out-breath itself continuing as exhalation of *awareness* – reaching down from the abdomen through our legs, and reaching down to very ground beneath our feet and below.

The Primary Freedom – Any action undertaken without taking time to be aware of *alternative possible actions* is not a *free* action. For free action, in principle, implies *choice* – which in turn requires awareness of alternative possible actions. **The Primary Practice** – *taking time to be aware* – is thus a precondition of freedom – allowing us to be aware of and choose between more than one possible action – rather than just *reacting* from or to our experience in an automatic, impulsive or controlling way – and without any awareness of alternative choices. **The Primary Choice** – to identify with pure awareness – is the precondition for exercising the freedom which that awareness brings – liberating us from bondage to unaware identifications and patterns of action, giving us time to be aware of alternative actions, and thus allowing us time to freely choose between them.

The Primary Delusion – This is the historic Western delusion, transcended in Eastern thought, that awareness is necessarily the *private property* of individual selves or 'subjects' – or a mere by-product of their bodies and brains. In reality all beings are but *individualised* expressions and embodiments of a *universal* awareness of which all things and being are a manifestation.

The Primary Reality – The most primordial reality and 'fact' of all is not the objective existence of a universe of bodies in space and time but a subjective awareness of such a universe. Just as dreaming cannot, in principle, be reduced to or explained by any particular thing we dream *of* – nor can awareness *as such* be reduced to a property or function of any force or energy, being or body we are aware *of* – whether in the waking or dream state. Space and time themselves are dimensions not of objective but of subjective reality – of awareness as such. Just as there can be nothing outside' space or 'before' time so there can be nothing *outside of or before awareness*. Awareness is the primary and absolute reality.

Awareness Based Cognitive Therapy
- a Case Report

Awareness Based Cognitive Therapy is a new form of therapeutic 'psycho-education', both verbal and non-verbal. Specifically it is 'education in awareness' through the explanation of basic principles and practices of awareness. What follows, whilst not a complete case study in itself, is a vignette drawn from a series of eight therapy sessions with a client. The purpose of the vignette is to offer an example of the type of therapeutic *outcomes* that therapists and counsellors – of whatever orientation or training background – can achieve in a short space of time, simply through introducing their clients to some of the primary principles and practice of awareness that form the foundation of Awareness Based Cognitive Therapy.

The client was a woman in her mid-thirties. She came because she felt that her constant worrying, anxiety and panic attacks threatened to destroy her life and deprive her of her job. She said she had lost her sense of self since leaving university, was not aware of her body and felt easily overwhelmed by disturbing thoughts and emotions. In addition she suffered from sleep disturbances and loss of appetite. No longer having any confidence in herself and her abilities she felt that her life wasn't worth living anymore.

The following 'Primary Principles and Practices of Awareness' were introduced, in the following order, over a period of 8 full therapy sessions and a 9th termination and feedback session.

The Primary Exercise – standing or sitting (1) be aware of your head, chest and entire upper body above the waist (2) be aware of the ground beneath your feet, your legs and entire lower body below the waist (3) sense the inner space of your lower abdomen or 'hara' and centre your awareness at a point deep down within it – a few inches below and behind the navel. This is your spiritual and physical centre of gravity.

The Primary Centre – a centre of both awareness and breathing in the lower abdomen, called 'hara' in Japanese. Seating our awareness and breathing in this still and silent 'hara' centre prevents us identifying with our head *or* hearts, mind *or* emotions.

Outcome: The client became aware that despite all the worries and anxieties, thoughts and emotions which upset her there was a womb-like space inside her – the *hara* – where she could experience peace and stillness. She repeated the exercise between sessions and reported that through this practice she could enter that space and centre herself in it within a very short time whenever she needed to calm herself down and come to rest in herself.

The Primary Equations – (1) every mental-emotional state is at the same time a bodily or somatic state, and can be sensed *as such* through the cultivation of heightened bodily awareness (2) we are as much aware of our being or self *as a whole* as we are aware of our *body* as a whole (both upper and lower body) and the space around it.

The Primary Breath Cycle – (1) always *begin* each in-breath using the abdominal muscles alone, feeling the abdomen pushing and expanding like a balloon – and in doing so filling it with *awareness* (2) as each out-breath comes to an end feel it extending itself as a downward flow of *awareness* through your legs to the very ground beneath our feet and below.

Note: because the client was very exhausted at the beginning of the session the exercise was done lying down, with the suggestion to sense the flow of awareness through her legs coming out through the soles of her feet.

Outcome: The client's first remark was "I've got legs! I didn't know that." She also noticed how she felt her head as being disconnected from her chest through a tightness in her throat, neck and shoulders, and how her shoulders were held high and tight, and how her entire chest in turn felt disconnected from her abdomen and lower body as a whole. The client also practiced the breathing cycle between sessions and reported a loosening of her shoulders and neck. For the first time ever she could feel her shoulder blades touching the mattress, which was a great surprise and joy for her. These were the beginnings of a greater awareness of her body as a whole – and with it, her self or being as a whole

The Primary Recognition – recognising that the *awareness* of any thing or thought, impulse or emotion we experience is *not itself* a thing or thought, impulse or emotion – and therefore is innately *free* of any thing or thought, impulse or emotion.

Outcome: The client began to be aware of thoughts as thoughts – and not as realities or facts. She also became aware that any given thought was just one way of mentally interpreting and expressing how she felt in her body. Recognising too, that her feelings were also shaped and affected by her thoughts, she realised that another, different thought might be a more *helpful* and less emotionally disturbing expression of how she was feeling, or of how she interpreted any experience, event or situation.

The Primary Choice – to identify with whatever we are experiencing (for example a situation, person, event, thought or emotion) or to identify with the pure *awareness* of experiencing it.

Outcome: the client first of all became aware that the habit of identifying with her thoughts fuelled her worrying and her distress. The real revelation for her was a recognition that her worries themselves *were essentially just thoughts* she was aware of, thoughts that she could choose to let go of rather than identify with. This awareness of her thoughts enabled her to evaluate their emotional effects and when necessary reformulate them as mental words. For example, the thought that 'I will never be able to do X next week' turned into 'I've done X well before and it is possible that I will do it well again'. Similarly, the thought 'There will never come a time when I feel well' changed into 'There is a possibility that I might change'. In these ways the client experienced the Primary Recognition and the Primary Choice as empowering Principles. Despite continuing to have worrying thoughts, she no longer felt helplessly emotionally distressed or overwhelmed by them. Practicing the Primary Choice in her everyday life, both at work and at home, helped her to feel calmer as well as more empowered, and considerably reduced her attacks of anxiety. She also reported that she got to sleep more easily – no longer finding herself just lying in bed worrying.

The Primary Practice – to 'meditate'. This does not mean 'doing' anything but rather taking short intervals of time for 'not doing' after each and every daily task, activity or focus of awareness – rather than just 'going from one thing to another' throughout the day and only taking time to rest or reflect at the end. In particular The Primary Practice means *taking time to be aware* – coming to rest in an *unfocussed* state of awareness in which we can (a) give ourselves time to sense in our bodies where what we have just been doing or focussing on has left us, whilst at the same time (b) once again becoming aware *more* of our bodies, selves, lives, environment and world *as a whole*. In this way we create 'breathing spaces' of awareness in which we recuperate ourselves, allow new insights to come to light and enable ourselves to choose what to do or focus on next in an aware way rather than an automatic or robotic way.

Outcome: previously the client had moved from one task or activity to the next without ever coming back to herself. Now she paused between tasks, creating a 'breathing space for awareness' in which she could again come to rest in her 'hara', feel her body and self as a whole and also take in the entire space around her. This made her feel less rushed and less tense – her time-space being no longer constricted by the habit of 'going from one thing to another'.

The Primary Sense – sensing our body surface and the entire space around it as a space of pure awareness, and feeling ourselves breathing this clear space or 'air' of awareness through every pore of our skin.

Outcome: the client realised that her awareness had been so focussed on her own thoughts and emotions and preoccupied with what was going on inside her, that she hadn't given much attention either to the space around her, or to the people in it. To her surprise she noticed how many people around her actually looked as worried or anxious as she herself felt inside. This helped her to no longer feel herself as so different from others – as an 'outsider'. In addition she was shocked to realise that she had been so inwardly preoccupied that she was not even aware of the actual living space she occupied (her boyfriend's flat) and just how uncomfortable she felt there. It was not a space which she felt was hers – and not just because she hadn't yet 'made it hers' by surrounding herself with her own things. The result was an agreement with her boyfriend to seek a flat they could share and whose space they could both feel as their own.

The Primary Stance – to fully feel and fully affirm everything we are aware of experiencing, 'positive' or 'negative', whilst at the same time distinguishing it from the pure awareness of experiencing it – and *identifying* with that very awareness.

Outcome: this helped the client to no longer feel guilty about who she was or what and how she was feeling. In not just acknowledging but affirming all she felt – without judging any feelings as positive or negative – she became aware of a greater richness of experiencing.

Summary: over the course of 8 weeks the client had reported improvements in many areas of her life. Her anxieties and worrying were reduced. She not only got to sleep more easily but reported that she actually slept *well* – and also that her appetite had returned. She had also begun to look for a new living space with her boyfriend.

Significantly for this particular client, she also reported being able for the first time in years to attend and enjoy social gatherings with others at the weekend, feeling herself fully 'present' rather than worrying about potential disasters that might occur at work over in the next week – such as making mistakes that might lead her to feeling and being seen as a failure, and thus possibly losing her job.

In the 9th session the client summed up her own progress by saying that even though she still found herself worrying occasionally she now felt she had been given *all the tools she needed* to ensure a less anxious life – and that she would continue to use them. She said she felt a lot more confident as a person and was looking forward to living her life in a much more relaxed and enjoyable way.

Although this client had not come specifically for a program or short-term 'course' in Awareness Based Cognitive Therapy, the elements of it that were introduced to her undoubtedly played a significant role in her progress over the eight sessions. This was partly due to her diligence in recalling and practicing what she learned in between sessions. Whilst such diligence cannot necessarily be expected from all or even most counselling or therapy clients, the foundational 'contract' for clients explicitly entering into a course of Awareness Based Cognitive Therapy includes a commitment to such inter-sessional practice – above all in the concrete relational and existential context of their everyday life-world. This is something quite different from just 'practicing' with such aids as instructional or meditational CDs or DVDs.

Part 5

Awareness and the Meaning of 'Depression'
from the word to a widened awareness

CONTENTS

fore-word

This article aims to undermine and deconstruct the psychiatric understanding of 'depression' as the presence of some 'thing' in need of treatment or management. In direct contrast, I present an account of depression that understands it as rooted, not in the presence of some 'thing' but in its absence – in a felt but still unformed awareness of a missing or lost dimension of our lives, a 'no-thing'.

In the annals of the psychiatric literature, the term 'depression' is used thousands if not millions of times, as if it were some 'thing' in no further need of explication – and without the question ever being raised as to what this 'thing' called 'depression' essentially *is*? Yet at the same time psychiatric explanations of 'depression' and authoritative professional guidelines to its 'treatment' or 'management' abound. This essay is designed to remind us of the simple truth made clear by the German thinker Martin Heidegger:

> **"All explanation presupposes a clarification of the essence of what it is that is supposed to be explained ... What good is all explaining if what has to be explained remains unclear?"**

what's in a word?

If a salesman or Jehovah's Witness comes to the door we already have an idea of how they will speak – as if reading aloud from a script, or by simply citing scripture. We actually hear and feel the way in which they are not actually using words to express themselves as individuals so much as engaging in a type of ventriloquy – letting Biblical words speak for and in place of them. Yet it is not just sellers of wares or scriptures that do so. Doctors, psychiatrist, business people and professionals of all sorts are often so immersed in their own professional languages, jargons and terminologies that in a certain way they inhabit these languages – live in them. In front of the Jehovah's Witness many non-Christians might feel awkwardly stuck for a simple yes-or-no answer when asked if they believe that God exists, or that Jesus was the 'Son of God'. This stuckness does not necessarily mean they don't have their own beliefs about religion. Instead, it has more to do with a question hidden or concealed by the question put to them. The question I mean is what *words* such as 'God' and 'Son of God' actually *mean* – both in general and to the particular person posing or answering questions about them? The trap concealed in such questions is the all-too-common assumption that we all already know – without any further ado and without any deeper questioning – what words such as 'God' mean. What this assumption rules out in advance is any question of how we or others understand and experience the meaning of words in general – whether religious words such as 'God', scientific words such as 'energy', or psychiatric terms such as 'depression' etc. It is simply *assumed* that words refer to some pre-given thing or being whose nature we all agree on. Thus even to give a yes-or-no answer to such seemingly simple question as 'Does God exist?' or 'Is this person suffering from 'depression?' is to collude with this assumption – the assumption that we all already know what it is we are talking about when such words or terms as 'God' or 'depression' – or any other word or term – is used. That assumption goes hand in hand with the assumption that language is itself just some 'thing' – a mere tool which we use to speak and express ourselves. It is true that we use language to name and describe, express and explain things. Yet language itself is no 'thing' – reducible to a set of sounds, letters or words. Nor is it just a tool we use to speak. For each of us has a particular language and vocabulary, one that just as much speaks *for* us as the language of a salesman or Jehovah's Witness.

We do not just speak words, using them as tools to express our ideas and experiences. Words themselves also *speak us* – *shaping and colouring the very ideas and experiences we think we are simply using them to 'express'.* So whether faced with a salesman, doctor, counsellor or psychiatrist we should always be aware of the question 'who speaks?' or 'who is speaking?' For the answer is often *not* the person actually speaking but *language* – the words that a person lives in and lives by – and the 'things' that they unquestioningly take these words to refer to. The whole authority of medical professionals in particular rests on our assuming that they *know what it is they are talking about* when they use their medical terms – when in reality they are the very last people to even begin to question the *meaning* of these words, so well-trained have they been in just seeing the world through these words. Their world-view, like everyone else's – is a 'word-view'.

the thing with words

Society quite literally 'has a thing' with words. The 'thing' is, no sooner has some new word or term been coined and become common currency in everyday language than we assume it refers to some 'thing' that has *always* existed – even before we had a word for it. So it is with the word 'depression', which is not just taken as a way of feeling, a subjective state or a set of symptoms but used to denote some object or 'thing in itself' – a 'disease entity'. Paradoxically, the very 'things' we think we have clearly and cleanly circled with words only become 'things' through the act of circling them – of running word-rings around them. Thus 'feeling depressed' becomes the symptom of some 'thing' called 'depression'. Doctors and psychiatrists then explain this thing in terms of some *other* thing such as a serotonin deficiency in the brain. A practitioner of 'complementary medicine' on the other hand, would search their own vocabulary or 'word-world' for the explanation – coming up with a phrase such as 'vitamin deficiency', 'energy blockage' or 'lack of chi'. Similarly, a shaman or witch-doctor might say that a depressed person was possessed by a malign 'spirit' of some sort or the victim of a curse. When it was the word of The Church that ruled large parts of world, it was the *universally accepted norm* to understand all illness as payment for past sins. And just as in some supposedly 'primitive' societies it still is the norm to blame symptoms on malign spirits, so does our supposedly 'rational' and 'scientific' culture blame many illnesses on harmful bacteria or viruses – even though our bodies are full of them all the time.

'word-worlds'

The worlds that most people live and work in are not made of concrete and glass, bricks and mortar, but of words. Doctors and psychiatrists for example, don't just work in surgeries or hospitals. Cleaners or hospital caterers do that. Doctors and psychiatrists, on the other hand, work within a world of *words* – the 'word-world' of medical terms, labels and explanations. And it is this word-world of their work that *rules* their work.

For most people the limits of their *language* are, as the philosopher Wittgenstein suggested, the limits of their *world*. That's why feelings or questions that they can't express in words may feel to them as 'unworldly' – so much so that they might even end up trying to explain them as something caused by hidden or unworldly beings – by extra-terrestrials, secret governmental agencies or evil or demonic spirits. The fact that a feeling can't be immediately expressed in words leaves them with a question. Yet instead of giving themselves time to feel the feeling itself *as* a wordless question, and to find their own words for that question, they grasp for words which provide an explanation of the feeling. In this way they come up with ready-made *answers* for why they are feeling the way they are – yet without having begun to ask themselves what *question or questions* it is that may lurk behind those feelings. In a word – people use words to come up with answers without first of all finding words for the questions they are feeling. They do this by circling things with ready-made or off-the-shelf words and phrases drawn from different established languages or vocabularies – different 'word worlds'. It doesn't matter which word-world the words they circle their feeling and experiences with come from – whether that of psychiatry, some area of medical science, some form of psychotherapy or some type of 'complementary' medicine. The process is the same.

the medical word-world

Psychiatrists and doctors in particular are paid to circle or pigeon-hole things in words – in diagnostic categories for example. If the experience of a large enough number of people nevertheless *defies* classification in terms of existing, neatly separated diagnostic categories – for example the separation of 'Depression' from 'Anxiety' – then all that medical professionals do is create a new term (for example 'Depressive Anxiety') with which they can continue to comfortably and authoritatively encircle or 'ring-fence' those people's experience. In this way, not just new words and terms but whole new *word-worlds* are eventually created. Modern science, not least in the form of 'scientific' medicine and psychiatry are characterised by jargon-filled 'scientific' word-worlds that bear little relation to the words used in previous eras to understand the nature of health and illness. These scientific word-worlds and their vocabularies of word-circles are treated today in exactly the same way as the Word of the Bible and of The Church used to be – as *unquestionable* representations or symbols of truth.

In the past, doctors who 'diagnosed' a patient's symptoms as signs of such a 'thing' – a hidden disease entity that was 'causing' them – were regarded by the rest of their profession as unprofessional quacks. Nowadays it is the other way round. A doctor not able to diagnose and label and 'test' for a possible disease entity such as 'cancer' (or 'depression') would be regarded both by himself, the patient and others doctors, as a failure. And it would be doctors who did *not* seek simply to diagnose or label a disease, but instead gave himself themselves time to *listen* longer and more deeply to the words of their patients themselves – taking heed of how *they* described their inwardly felt 'dis-ease' – who would be regarded as unprofessional quacks.

Not having time to listen however, today's doctors often diagnose patients whose symptoms or dis ease they can't pigeon-hole as suffering from a 'thing' called 'depression'. Or if depressive or anxious feelings are the very symptoms that a patient 'presents' with, they are either dosed with medications or packed off to counsellors or psychologists who will actually have a bit more time to listen, and with whom patients can then talk 'about' those feelings. In practice this often means receiving a short-course, quick-fix course of 'thought correction' of the sort now pompously termed 'cognitive therapy'. This is based on the belief that depressive *feelings* have nothing to do with negative aspects of the real world but are nothing more than a result of unnecessary negative *thoughts* arising in response to that world.

'be-aware'

The message of this essay to anyone who believes or has been told they are suffering from a clinically diagnosed psychiatric condition or 'mental illness' of any sort is – beware. 'Beware' means 'be aware' – in particular be aware that just because there is an accepted diagnostic *word* for something does not mean there is actually some 'thing' corresponding to that word. If people are not sufficiently aware of this – they may all too easily become *trapped* in the word-circles and word-worlds of psychiatry and its diagnostic terms. And yet even if they avoid or manage to escape from the trap of *this* particular word-world, without this type of awareness, they might simply end up trapped in the word-worlds of some other form of medicine, psychotherapy or 'healing'.

Yet where would we be without such word-worlds, religious or scientific? Would we not simply be left again with the seemingly unanswerable question of how to find words for wordless dimensions of our feeling experiences of the world? It is because all of us face this question in one way or another that we all make use of words to circle and make sense of our wordless experience of ourselves and the world around us.

Is there any way out of entrapment in word-circles and word-worlds, besides running from one to another, and in this way quite literally running around in – within – different word-circles and word-worlds? Yes there is. *It is the way of the poet and thinker* rather than the officially sanctioned priest, healer, psychiatrist or 'scientist'. For true poets and thinkers don't instantly 'run rings' around their experience with 'word circles' drawn from their own unquestioned 'word-worlds'. Instead they look for – or rather patiently await and *feel for* – their own words. Their aim is to create a *word-world* that truly expresses *their* world, as *they* actually sense, feel and experience it on a wordless level. Or else they patiently feel for and seek to formulate – in their own words – the deeper *questions* they sense lurking within their own experience and their own feelings. We do not need to be poets and thinkers to do this, but we can follow their example in seeking our own words for our own experiential and emotional worlds.

Of course ultimately nobody 'owns' words – for by their nature they are not private property but part of a shared language. From this point of view it may appear to make no sense to speak of poets and thinkers finding their 'own' words for their experience of the world – *unless* we mean only that they are not letting themselves be trapped and encircled within the rigid boundaries of unquestioned but officially recognised *word-worlds* i.e. terminologies and jargons of any sort – spiritual or scientific, medical or psychiatric. Beware then – *be aware* – of words, of the unquestioned word-worlds they belong to – and of the word-circles they can entrap *your* unique world of feelings and experiences in.

the word 'depression'

The word 'depression' derives from the Latin verb *depressus*, past participle of *deprimere* (to press down, weigh down, dig down or dig deep). As a noun, the word 'depression' means 'a deepening, a 'digging down', 'pressing down' or 'weighing down'.

de- (down, away) and *premere* (to press)

'Depression' is one word belonging to a family of everyday nouns, verbs and phrases that include deep, depth, pressure, suppression and oppression, to oppress or suppress, to press or pressure, or to feel pressed or pressured. It was only in the 1950's that doctors and psychiatrists first started to use the word 'depression' to denote some 'thing' – firstly a classified psychiatric disorder, and secondly the 'thing' that was its supposed cause – a purely hypothetical, invisible and still *unverifiable* deficiency in the brain of a 'neurotransmitter' called 'serotonin'.

If someone says that they feel heavy, fatigued, drawn or 'weighed down' by the pressures of life we know what they mean. That is because the words they use speak for themselves in a vocabulary of the *senses* – their own directly felt sense of themselves. The same applies if people speak of being in a 'dark' or 'black mood', of falling into a 'black hole', or of seeing no 'light' at the end of the tunnel. Here again they are using a vocabulary of the senses – in this case of light and darkness. That does not mean that the words or phrases they employ are just 'metaphors'. People who feel depressed really do feel an *inner* darkness, blackness, weight or heaviness in themselves.

For the medical and psychiatric professions however, how people actually sense themselves and their bodies from within – *subjectively* – is not what it's all about. Instead it has to be explained by some hidden 'thing' – an *object* that is 'causing' them to feel that way. This view lends itself to medical treatments aimed at 'removing' this object – even though it is essentially no object or 'thing' at all but a subjective way of feeling.

Unless people are prepared to acknowledge meaning in the way they feel, they will be tempted to look for ways to mentally negate 'negative' feelings or medicate them away. That itself is a paradox, for feelings as such are no more 'positive' or 'negative' than colours. What we call a 'negative' feeling is really a feeling we would rather not feel and therefore actively seek to *negate* in different way, whether by simply suppressing it, or experiencing it as a generalised state that is then labelled as 'anxiety' or 'depression'. And paradoxical though it may sound, the most 'positive', freeing and empowering response to any 'negative' feeling is precisely *not* to negate it but instead to positively affirm it; not to try and free oneself of it but to freely and decisively *choose* to feel it – indeed to choose to feel it even more strongly rather than less, and attending principally to where and how one feels it in one's body. For the self or 'I' that proactively and positively *chooses* to feel a 'negative' feeling is distinct – in principle – from that 'I' which merely suffers or feels overwhelmed by that feeling, or is so identified with it ('I'-dentified) that it cannot, in principle, become free of it.

the medical denial of meaning

After the 2nd World War a concentration camp survivor called Victor Frankl wrote a book drawn from his observation that those who bore the ongoing psychological and physical trauma of the camps best were those who sought, found or felt that there was still *meaning* in their lives. As a result Frankl disputed the idea that the human being was driven either by sex drives or by a will to 'be happy' and argued instead that happiness was a mere by-product of that deeper drive that he called 'The Will to Meaning'.

As we have seen, the word 'depressed' is part of a word family that includes the words deep and depth. Could it not be that language itself is trying to tell us something here – namely that 'depression' itself might have a deeper *meaning* – not as a mere disorder of the brain but as a specific way of *feeling* that tends to lead us back down into the innermost depths of our *being*. Underlying the whole 'medical model' approach to both 'mental' and 'physical' illness however is a basic belief which can be seen as the most sacred dogma of modern medicine. This is the belief that any sort of symptom or felt 'dis-ease' has no deeper *meaning* – except as a sign of some medically recognised *disease*. That is why medical professionals make no attempt whatsoever to explore the personally felt meaning or 'sense' of a patient's symptoms. For this would require them to inquire much more about the life context in which they first emerged and to seek to make sense of them in that context. Instead doctors and psychiatrists take symptoms merely as diagnostic 'signs' or 'signifiers' of some 'thing' – the mysterious 'disease entity' again. Every symptom has meaning or significance to them only in terms of some already signified *medical* sense. The doctor's medical catalogue of already *signified senses* (potential 'diagnoses') rules out from the start any way of helping a patient explore or understand the *sensed significance* of their symptoms – the meaning or sense they themselves might personally feel or discover in them. This replacement of directly felt sense or significance with already labelled or signified senses belongs to the very essence of the medical-model approach both to somatic and 'mental' illness or 'disorders' – not least 'depression',

the depression 'thing'

Most people know what it means if someone says they "feel depressed". They know it from their own experience. That 'knowing' is therefore innately 'scientific', since it is 'evidence-based' or 'empirical' in the most direct sense – coming from the direct evidence of people's immediate *sense* of themselves, a sense that takes the tangible form of sensations such as feeling pressed or weighed down, heavy, dark etc.

'Feeling depressed' then, is a self-evident subjective experience that no one can deny or invalidate – and that no medical tests are needed to 'prove'. To take it as a sign of some *thing* called 'depression' is quite *another* thing however. And to then explain *that* 'thing' as a product of some *other* thing that a person does *not* feel or experience directly (a defective gene or lack of serotonin in the brain for example) is not 'evidence-based' science in any sense of the term but *medical mystification*. It does not 'make sense' of depressive symptoms but quite literally makes 'non-sense' of them – attributing them to some 'thing' that is not actually sensed at all, like a serotonin deficiency in the brain – itself something scientifically unverified.

Arguing that depression is caused by a lack of serotonin or some other neurotransmitter is like arguing that just because cocaine gives people a high and makes them feel good, feeling low or depressed 'proves' that they *lack cocaine in the brain*. Diagnosing people who *feel* depressed as suffering from a 'thing' called 'depression', and then prescribing them legal drugs (so-called SSRI's or 'selective-serotonin-reuptake-inhibitors' such as Prozac) is therefore like prescribing people illegal drugs such as cocaine. In fact, from the evidence of the awful, acute and often chronic side-effects of such 'legal' drugs it is far *worse*. The fact that this evidence is not merely 'anecdotal' (such a useful word in 'scientifically' dismissing the *evidence* of so many patient's actual experience) is proved by the bizarre paradox that pharmaceutical companies are legally bound to warn users of 'anti-depressants' that their side effects might include *suicidal thoughts*. Unfortunately this warning has proved all too true in far too many cases – not least in the form of countless actual suicides or acts of self-harm violence towards others.

prejudicial words

Society officially frowns on the use of illegal drugs – whether 'uppers' or 'downers' – even whilst pharmaceutical companies make huge profits from the legal prescription of both types of drug in the treatment of 'mental illnesses'. Society also officially frowns on the stigma attached to 'mental illness' and on prejudice or discrimination towards them – not least those suffering from the variety of 'disorders' known as 'depression'. Yet we need only consider everyday words and phrases to see how this prejudice is part of everyday language use itself. Just as in Orwell's famous book 'Animal Farm', the slogan of the revolutionary pigs (later reversed) was 'Four legs good. Two legs bad', so in ordinary language can we find a hidden slogan: **'Up is good. Down is Bad'**. This slogan takes many different forms, for example **'High is good. Low is bad.'** This message finds expression in countless common phrases:

*Feeling **low**' (bad), 'a **high** point' (good), 'a **low** point' (bad), '**high** status' (good), '**low** status' (bad), 'a record **high**' (good), 'a record **low**' (bad), 'going **up** in the world' (good) 'going **down** in the world' (bad), 'coming **up** with something' (good) 'coming **down** with something' (bad), 'standing **up** for something or someone' (good), 'standing **down**' or 'letting someone **down**' (bad), to '**up**grade' (good), to '**down**grade' (bad), '**up**turn' (good), '**down**turn', (bad), '**up**beat' (good), '**down**beat'(bad) etc.*

Whilst the cliché goes that everyone has their 'ups and downs' in life, the linguistic prejudice remains that **'Up is good'** and **'Down is bad'**. 'Heaven' itself is seen as 'up' there in the 'highest' spheres, whereas Hell is seen as 'down below' in the lowest depths. Here we find a hint of yet more slogans or mantra concealed within language itself: **'Above is good. Below is bad'. 'Rising is good. Falling is bad'**. Thus we **rise up** into the heights of success or Heaven itself, whereas we fall into the depths of Hell or failure – for 'to fail' is a verb whose root meaning is 'to fall'. Given all this prejudicial language it is no wonder that people find it difficult to admit to feeling 'low' or 'down' or 'depressed' – let alone extremely depressed – and may indeed feel all the *more* 'depressed' just for feeling 'low' or 'down' in the first place. For just doing so is to go against the prejudicial grain of language that tells us that 'Up is good. Down is bad', 'High is good. Low is bad' – thus making people who feel 'bad' or 'low' not only 'feel bad' but feel *bad* – as if they were literally *lowdown* 'losers' or 'failures'.

whatever happened to 'melancholy'?

In the past 'depression' was referred to in the West as 'melancholy' or 'melancholia'. Melancholy itself was understood as one of the four basic 'temperaments' (the sanguine, phlegmatic, choleric and melancholic) that made up human nature, and each of which could be a more or less dominant element in each individual's make up. The term melancholy comes from two Greek words (*melas* and *kholē*) which meant 'black bile' – this being one of the four basic substances or 'humors' to be found in the human body. As a temperament or humor, melancholy was acknowledged as an intrinsic and basic aspect of *human nature* and of the human body, corresponding both to one of the four humours, to one of the four elements of nature (earth) and to one of the four seasons (autumn). Unlike 'depression', melancholy was not simply seen as something alien to the human being, human body and human nature – an *unnatural* bodily disorder or dysfunction of mind in need of 'treatment'. Similarly, in India, the symptoms associated with 'depression' were understood as expressions of 'tamas' – this being one of three basic and natural qualities or 'gunas' of the soul, also associated with the colour black, along with feelings of inertia, lethargy, heaviness, and darkness of mood. Though the symptoms of melancholy or 'melancholia' as a 'disease' or 'distemper' have been recognised by physicians for millennia, since Aristotle onwards it has *also* been associated with great achievement, creative genius and deep wisdom. Indeed the 19th century philosopher Friedrich Schelling wrote of "the deep, indestructible melancholy of all life." Similarly, perhaps the greatest 20th century philosopher – Martin Heidegger – wrote that philosophy as such was founded in a "fundamental mood" of melancholy.

It was Freud however, who presented the first modern and purely psychological analysis of melancholy, in his essay entitled

'Mourning and Melancholia' (1915). In this essay Freud compares and contrasts the nature of mourning and melancholia.

> "It is well worth noticing that, although mourning involves grave departures from the normal attitude to life, it never occurs to us to regard it as a pathological condition and refer it for medical treatment. We rely on it being overcome after a certain lapse of time, and we look upon any interference with it as useless or even harmful. The distinguishing mental features of melancholia are a profoundly painful sense of dejection, a cessation of interest in the outside world, loss of capacity to love, inhibition of all activity ... a lowering of the self-regarding feelings to a degree that finds utterance in self-reproaches and self-revilings, and culminates in a delusional expectation of punishment."

The thesis of Freud's essay is that melancholia is similar to mourning, being fundamentally a response to a grievous experience of *loss*. What distinguishes mourning and melancholia however, is that "In mourning the world has become impoverished and empty, during melancholia, it is the ego itself." That is because in melancholia, the ego experiences its feelings of loss not as the loss of an 'object' – something other than self such as another person – but rather as a loss of self. In contrast therefore, to the process of mourning arising from acute awareness of loss through separation or bereavement, melancholia arises essentially from a denial or *lack of awareness* of something lost or absent in one's life and soul.

> "One cannot see clearly what it is that has been lost, and it is all the more reasonable to suppose that the patient cannot consciously perceive what he has lost either. This, indeed, might be so even if the patient is aware of the loss

that has given rise to his melancholia, but only in the sense he knows *whom* he has lost but not *what* he has lost in him. This would suggest that melancholia is in some way related to an object-loss which is withdrawn from consciousness, in contradistinction to mourning, in which there is nothing about the loss that is unconscious."

People suffer from *unaware* feelings of loss or absence of all sorts – loss or absence of love and understanding, of an authentic sense of self, of lasting and fulfilling relationships – and last but not least, a feeling of connection with the universe and with the divine. Freud's fundamental distinction between mourning and melancholia sheds light on an important characteristic of 'depression' as a *feeling* rather than as a 'disease entity'. For whereas in mourning the mourner might, through completing a process of grieving, eventually come to find renewed meaning in the world of human life and relationships, the depressed person is 'shadowed' by a sense of loss or absence of *meaning* which (quite literally) nothing in the *world* can make up for – for it is not consciously bound up with the loss of some easily identifiable thing or person.

As a result, the individual experiences a fundamental loss or absence in their sense of self, what Freud termed 'the ego'. "Thus, the shadow of the object fell upon the ego, and … object-loss was transformed into an ego-loss." In response, and unlike the mourner, the melancholic becomes ever-more 'narcissistically' self-oriented – in an attempt to *be* that which fills their own sense of an inner void or absence, or else to *obtain* it from the world. For we live in a world dominated by an egotistic and narcissistic culture in which consumer commodities are presented as essential foundations to or enhancements of our sense of self, as well as boosts to our social status and self-esteem. Indeed people actually speak of 'retail therapy'. Both retail commodities and psychiatric medications have today become the principal, culturally 'prescribed' means of filling a felt void or absence at the heart of our soul or psyche, and of maintaining a connection with the world in the face of loss or absence – not however, the real world of living human relationships but a world of material commodities and medical treatments. This is a world far removed from the values of freedom, creative achievement and philosophical wisdom hitherto seen as latent in the mood of melancholy itself – not despite but through its burdens.

> "Freedom is only to be found where there is a burden to be shouldered. In creative achievements this burden always represents an imperative and a need that weighs heavily upon man's mood, so that he comes to be in a mood of melancholy. All creative action resides in a mood of melancholy, whether we are clearly aware of the fact or not, whether we speak at length about it or not. All creative action resides in a mood of melancholy, but this is not to say that everyone in a melancholy mood is creative."

> Martin Heidegger

depression and 'no-thing-ness'

A famous German poet once wrote: 'Where word breaks off no thing may be." Reversing this motto it would read: "Where thing breaks off no word may be." 'Depression', though it is itself a word is essentially a *wordless* state – sometimes leading an individual into a total speechlessness or muteness. Whence this wordlessness or speechlessness? One important reason is that whilst we have words for things that are actually there – present – we don't have words for the *feeling* of something or someone *not* being there, for a sense of *absence*. Similarly we don't have words for an absent or unthought

thought or an absent or unfelt feeling. Just as we also don't have words for an absent sense of self or of our own bodies – for a sense of being 'no one', 'nothing' or 'nobody'. With this in mind, it is worth asking if the whole idea of 'depression' as some 'thing' – one that can in turn be explained by other things – might not be the very *opposite* of the truth, or rather its mirror image? For what if, in contrast to this idea, the very essence of depression lies precisely in a felt *absence* of something or someone, or alternatively in the experience of being mistreated or abused as a mere 'thing' or 'body' – and thus effectively treated as 'nothing' and 'nobody'? This would account for the way in which 'depression', far from being a 'mental' state or mental 'illness', is a state which pervades our entire felt body, in this way helping us to feel our own *self* more fully – not just as a bodiless mind but in a fully embodied way, as 'some-body'. It would also account for the close relation between the depression and *mourning* – for though we may name the person we have lost, the feeling of their *bodily* absence is not itself anything nameable – it just weighs or presses down on us, leaving us feeling 'de-pressed'. What 'presses' or 'weighs down' upon the 'de-pressed' person then is no 'thing' but the absence of something, an absence that, by its very nature, cannot be expressed in words.

Considerations like these make the very word 'depression' into a very paradoxical one of the sort that certain types of language theorist call a 'floating signifier'. This is a sign or symbol that is said to 'float' because it does not refer to or 'denote' any actual or definable thing – because there is nothing 'signified' by it. The same considerations also make the 'thing' that is called 'depression' into a very paradoxical sort of 'thing', being precisely a feeling or mood that serves to fills the empty gap or vacuum created by what is essentially a sense of nothingness or *no-thing-ness* – one that is not so much caused by some 'thing' so much as evoked by the *absence* of something – or by an absent sense of *being* someone and somebody.

Being someone – a self or 'subject' – is quite different from being a *mere* 'thing', a mere mental, emotional or physical 'object' for oneself or others. Yet in a culture dominated by the need to perceive things as objects and possess them as commodities, being a self or subject tends to be identified with conceiving and *perceiving* the world as a world of *objects*. So whilst our entire *experience* of ourselves and of reality is essentially something *subjective*, in this culture both science and medicine identify reality only with objects and 'objectivity' – reducing the body to a clinical object and the self itself to a mere fiction created by the brain. It would be surprising if, in such a culture, most people did *not* feel depressed. This applies particularly to those at the sharp end of this culture – people whose depression stems from being objects of political or economic oppression, or from the pressures of what Marx called 'wage slavery' – earning a living through producing objects for others. It applies also to people whose early relationships were ones in which they themselves were perceived or treated as mere objects of use and abuse.

the logic of 'depression'

When people feel 'low', 'down' or acutely or chronically 'depressed' for no apparent reason they naturally see no rhyme or reason in it. It confronts them – and is seen by doctors and psychiatrists – as an innately 'irrational' or 'illogical' state to be in, one that therefore needs to be mentally or 'cognitively' corrected ('cognitive therapy') and/or pharmaceutically treated with 'anti-depressants'. Older ways of seeking to understand the *meaning* of depression, such as those that evolved among psychoanalysts, have since been discarded as 'old hat' under the pressure of the pharmaceutical industry. Yet due to the ever-increasing costs of prescription drugs, medical psychiatrists today are beginning to acknowledge these older insights indirectly. Indeed some fashionable psychiatric trends have begun to bring them back in the much diluted and distorted form of supposedly 'new' theories, along with new forms of 'psychological' rather than purely pharmaceutical 'treatment'.

The term 'psychology', though it did not exist in ancient Greece, is derived from the Greek words 'psyche' and 'logos'. The Greek word 'logos' meant 'word', 'speech' or any form of spoken 'account'. It is from the Greek *logos* that the modern word 'logic' is derived.

What characterised the older psychoanalytic *logoi* or 'accounts' of depression was that they were derived from the word or *logos* of patients themselves rather than from the pseudo-scientific jargon of psychiatrists. Freud himself worked in this way, being the first to attend so closely to the word of the patient as to begin to hear its inner 'speech' or *logos* and discover an inner 'logic' to their symptoms. It was Freud who first began, in a way yet to be properly understood by today's psychiatrists, a wholly different type of 'logic' in the relation between *words* and *things* – a relation fundamental to *thinking* as such. His insights were taken up by others, in particular by Melanie Klein, Wilfred Bion and Donald Winnicott, in a way that led them to see in what they called 'the depressive position' something that had a healing and maturational value, enabling the individual to experience both self and other as 'whole' beings, rather than as things.

'transformations'

What follows is my interpretation, based on Bion's 'Theory of Thinking', of a sequence of 'psycho-logical' transformations that the psychoanalysts referred to above identified as occurring in the *absence* of some 'thing', transformations that lead all individuals to inwardly alternate, to one degree or another, between what Klein called a 'paranoid-schizoid' position on the one hand and a healthier 'depressive position' on the other.

1. the loss or *absence* of a good thing (for example the absence of the mother or breast for the infant) is felt as bad, or the experience of a bad thing leaves the individual with a feeling of absence (for example an absent feeling of being loved or worthy).

2. the experience of feeling bad through the *absence of a good thing* is experienced as the *presence of a bad thing*. Thus 'feeling bad' is experienced as a bad thing – a 'bad feeling' – rather than as the expression of an absent thing or 'no-thing'.

3. the incapacity to tolerate or contain 'bad feelings' that arise from experience of a 'no-thing' (for example the infant's experience of a 'no-breast') leads to those feelings being neither fully felt nor thought.

From this basic set of transformations a whole sequence of others can follow:

4. Incapacity to tolerate the frustration of absence – the 'no-thing' – leads to it not only being felt as a bad thing (a 'bad object' in analytic terms) but also gives rise to an intense need to identify the 'no-thing' with some actual thing or object – whether in the form of a person or place, a part of the body or any perceptible object, real or hallucinated.

5. The object having been a 'bad object', it is also a source of persecutory or paranoid fears, phobias and anxieties, being perceived as something that has done or might do bad things to the individual.

6. Externalising or 'projecting' bad internal bodily feelings into external objects of all sorts makes the individual feel more empty – more of a 'nothing' or 'nobody' than before.

7. Internalising or 'introjecting' those bad object or feelings makes the individual feel *they* are bad – and thus in fear of retribution by externalised bad objects.

8. Whichever way it goes, the individual's whole sense of being a self or 'subject' – their whole *identity* – becomes entirely dependent on a relationships to a 'bad object' – whether external or internal.

9. Real or imaginary *perceptions of concrete things* (including people) as good or bad objects becomes a substitute for the *conception of abstract thoughts*.

10. Some *thing* (whether in the form of an object or person, internal or external) is always sought as the cause or explanation for feeling bad. *Feeling bad* is always turned into a *bad feeling* towards that object and a persecutory fear of it. In this way a *fight-flight relation to* all 'bad feelings' – based on an absent sense of self and a generalised fear of absence or 'no-thing-ness' – replaces a *feeling* relation to others and a capacity to *think* with words.

What we call 'depression' is not itself a 'thing' – a disease entity – but a *process* that can serve to overcome this fight-flight relation to the 'no-thing', ultimately leading to the recovery of a fully embodied sense of self based on tolerance of bad feelings, and the capacity to represent and communicate in words a sense of absence or 'no-thing-ness'. For words and verbal thinking do *not arise* as representations of *things* but rather as 'placeholders' for their absence – for 'no-things'.

the nature of 'anxiety'

What is called 'anxiety' is essentially a *flight-flight* response to absence characterised by *paranoid* or *persecutory* feelings towards a 'no-thing'. Yet the types of anxiety or 'paranoid transformation' that take us, for example, from (1) 'feeling bad' to (2) labelling certain feelings *as* bad (3) seeing them as 'negative' or 'bad' feelings, and then (4) identifying these bad feelings with some thing and then (5) feeling this thing as bad – a 'bad object' – are nothing abnormal or unusual. Take for example 'writers' block' or difficulty in writing or communicating in words. These are related to fear of the 'no-thing' and the 'no-thought' – the emptiness of the blank page or 'blank mind'. Or take even a competent writer who is feeling 'bad' about (stuck, bored with or critical towards) a piece he or she is writing. The sense of 'feeling bad' towards the writing easily becomes turned into a 'bad feeling' – one which is not only felt as a thing in itself, but identified with and 'projected' into the piece of writing itself. It is then that the actual physical form of the writing, whether as a paper manuscript or a computer file, may be felt by the author as a 'bad object' – and avoided because of the bad feelings it has come to be identified with and symbolise.

Any person or place, thing or thought associated with feeling bad may come to be felt as a bad thing in itself – a 'bad object' to be avoided. Even an object initially felt as good, whether a person, place or part of the body, a type of food or a cherished belief, a once idolised figure or a mere item of furniture, can easily and even instantaneously be transformed into a 'bad object' through becoming a receptacle for bad feelings. Alternatively, people may alternate, sometimes very rapidly, between seeing a thing or person as a good or loved object and seeing them as a bad, feared or hateful object to be avoided or fought.

This 'splitting' of things and people into good and persecutory bad objects – which results also in a splitting of the self or subject – was one of the 'primary defences' against absence that Klein saw what she called "the depressive position" as overcoming, leading to a greater awareness of both self and other as whole beings, and a greater capacity to relate to them as such.

From this point of view 'anxiety' can also be understood both as a defence against the depressive position and at the same time as a potential threshold state to entering it. Anxiety is not accentuated but relieved by depressive states in which senses of absence or loss – the 'no-thing' can come to be fully felt, thought and communicated in words.

'the depressive position'

In essence, what Klein termed 'the depressive position' was less a 'position' than a *process*. And yet the direction of this process was such as to lead to what she called the depressive *position*. Implicit in her understanding and use of the term 'depressive position' however, is the suggestion of a specific 'place' or 'bearing' within ourselves from which we can come to experience both things and people in a more healthy, hale or 'whole' way – as *whole beings* rather than as more or less fragmented or integrated collections of parts –

and thus ultimately come to an awareness of reality as such as a singular whole or unity. Given this understanding of the term, it is odd that this 'position' should be described as 'depressive' in the first place (a word weighed with negative connotations) were it not for the fact that in Klein's view, the *process* of arriving at it was an on-going difficult and tenuous one requiring the surrender under pressure of psychological defences such as 'splitting' and 'projective identification', and the acceptance instead of feelings of loss, absence and ambivalence towards things and people previously or otherwise split into good or bad, loved or hated parts – what Klein called the 'paranoid-schizoid position'.

good reasons for feeling depressed

"Just because you're paranoid doesn't mean they're not out to get you."

It doesn't take much thought to realise that most of the real life reasons – *good reasons* – for people feeling depressed have to do with 'object loss', the loss of some 'thing'. This includes loss of jobs or income, loss of loved ones or relationships, loss of freedom or potential loss of life – that which ultimately confronts us all through death. Along with such losses may go a loss not just of happiness but of hope or health, a loss of trust or security, a loss of identity or sense of belonging, a loss of feeling and vitality, and last but not least a loss of meaning and of will – in particular the will to live. Suicide is not loss of self through self-inflicted death. On the contrary it results from an already lost sense of self – from a sense of already being dead – from which perspective continued life is felt as a form of living death, artificially sustained. Understanding the many *good reasons* why people might feel depressed provide us with all the *more reason* for not seeing or seeking the meaning of the word 'depression' in some actually present 'thing'. For at its heart is a sense of absence, loss and, ultimately, a felt dread of 'no-thing-ness' or 'non-being' that lurks at the very core of our being.

'depression' and 'dread'

What people experience as 'depression' is also expressed through the German word 'Angst' – usually translated as either 'anxiety' or 'dread'. The German philosopher Martin Heidegger had a lot to say about 'Angst'. His words echo in some ways the psychoanalytic viewpoint of Klein, but seek to go even deeper in exploring the essential nature and meaning of what we call 'depression' – not simply *as* depression, nor even as some new clinical category of 'depressive anxiety' (or some mere admixture of anxiety 'and' dread) but rather as 'Angst'. For this is a word which, precisely because there is no easily definable 'thing' through which it can be translated in conventional clinical terms, led Heidegger to see *nothingness* as its essence – in a way that corresponds also to what I have suggested may be the essential nature and meaning of what we call 'depression'...

"All things, and we with them, sink into indifference. But not in the sense that everything simply disappears. Rather, in the very drawing away from us as such, things turn toward us. This drawing away of everything in its totality, which in angst is happening all around us, haunts us. There is nothing to hold on to. The only thing that remains and comes over us – in this drawing away of everything –is this "nothingness."

As Jorn K. Bramann comments:

"That things do not "simply disappear" in the experience of *angst* is important. Things actually "turn toward us" [Klein's 'bad objects'] *as* things that are alien and uncanny. In the experience of *angst* things have, in fact, a peculiarly ominous presence ... Heidegger compares the experience of *angst* with the dread that we may feel in the dark: without light we see nothing, yet the feeling of dread arises precisely because things are present – somewhere out there, vaguely threatening, but without revealing any danger in particular. It is in this way that the totality of what exists remains present in the state of *angst*, even though we have the feeling that everything is "drawing away".

What Heidegger refers to as "nothingness," in other words, appears in the presence of things – in the presence of the world that has become thoroughly alien and "indifferent." This shows that the "nothingness" Heidegger talks about in ... is not anything like a physical void, but a void – as one might say – of sense, of significance, or of meaning." What sort of meaning? Bramann again:

"We have our more or less regular tasks, familiar routines, and customary expectations. People have their known occupations and places, and things their more or less traditional appearances and functions. Even if occasional changes take place with respect to this or that detail, the over-all nexus of activities, functions, and goals remains a more or less ordered environment, a familiar context. Ordinarily we are at home in an organized world. It is the feeling of being at home in such a familiar world that is suspended in the experience of *angst*: Ordinary objects look strange, everyday activities pointless, and common sense objectives outlandish. Encountering "nothingness" means to feel uncanny and dislodged in a perfectly familiar world. There are several reasons why Heidegger finds the experience of *angst* important. One of them is the fact that it brings us closer to an understanding of Being – of what it means to be ... For in the state of *angst* nothing particular matters anymore; everything in the world is equally indifferent to a person who is caught by this kind of dread ...Thus the only thing left is the pure "being-there" of everything, the baffling fact of the world's indifferent existence. This existence becomes the ultimate enigma for the person in *angst*; it prompts the wondering question: "Why is there anything at all – and not rather nothing?"

While this question is a gateway to Heidegger's inquiry into the nature of Being, it is also a way of approaching and coming to terms with the quality of one's own existence. The encounter with nothingness, according to Heidegger, puts me into a position where I can choose an authentic existence, or where otherwise I can allow myself to fall back into a sort of life where most things are decided by others, or by circumstances of a more or less impersonal nature. *Angst*, in other words, reveals to me my fundamental freedom. As ordinary individuals we are part of the world, and thus part of what "draws away" in the experience of *angst*. When seized by *angst* we become strangers to ourselves: our ordinary identities recede, and the everyday lives we live become as uncanny as the world around us. Suspended in *angst* I am not this or that person anymore, but an undefined being whose only characteristic is being-there. This pure being-there, according to Heidegger, is our most basic existence. In facing the nothingness revealed by *angst* all the activities I engage in and all the things I represent in everyday life fall away as so many roles and masks. In this "standing out into nothingness," as Heidegger puts it, I have a chance to make a new start, and to choose my life with a conscious resolve that had not been available to me in the routines of my ordinary everyday life. *Angst* is thus not necessarily a negative experience; it can be understood and seized as a precondition for waking up, for a personal liberation. In ordinary everyday life we tend to be locked into routine, and being preoccupied by practical tasks and busy with their execution we rarely question the sense of the whole system of cares, goals, and activities. To a much larger extent than we usually realize, the cares, goals, and activities that define our lives are determined by others instead of ourselves. I do what "one" is supposed to do; I have the goals in life that people generally have. I follow the herd, as some philosophers put it. It is, of course, not always wrong to do what others do. But it is one thing to do so because others do it, or to do it for specific and sound reasons. *Angst* relieves us, as it were, from our herd instinct and enables us to make our own personal decisions. *Angst* can be the means to become our own selves. By prompting us to become genuine individuals, it can make our lives authentic."

"The capacity to wonder and inquire, grounded in that distance, is a manifestation of a fundamental freedom, the freedom to conceive and re-conceive the world in many ways, and to change one's relation to it accordingly. Instead of being locked into a particular cultural tradition, for example, with its fixed and established ways of looking at and relating to things, human beings are endowed with the capacity to take a step back from everything and to look at the world at any time as if it were entirely new, i.e., strange. This capacity … is the basis for the possibility of taking a hold of one's life in a way no other kind of being has."

"Heidegger describes another way in which a person can encounter nothingness, and thereby take hold of his or her existence authentically: by facing death … Again, this is not accomplished by simply thinking about the matter, not even by very serious thinking. According to Heidegger it is only the *feeling* of *angst* that genuinely reveals nothingness – in this case the possible not-being of everything that I personally am. Only the *feeling* of *angst* reveals death as *my* death, the death that only I will die. And in doing so *angst* individualizes my existence, for the life that I live authentically is the life that is defined by my personal death."

"In an abstract way all people know, of course, that they are mortal, and that they can die at any moment. In ordinary life this knowledge tends to become diluted or diminished; most people suppress the awareness of their own possible death by keeping themselves occupied by all sorts of other things – comparatively trivial things for the most part ... The full awareness of my death brings my existence into a clear focus that is absent from the average sort of life that is frittered away on unimportant details and cluttered with superficial distractions. A conscious "being-toward-death" will encourage me to stop running with the herd, escape the anonymous dictates of what "one" is supposed to do, cease moving through life like a somnambulist--and actively take hold of my life with conscious resolve and deliberate determination. Facing my death in earnest provides me with the possibility to make my life truly my own, and thus authentic."

"When we stare out to the darkness or, more precisely, stare into the darkness, into the world of infinity, we see nothing – we grown-ups, we who are all-too grown up. But let us look into the darkness like the child we once were ... yes perhaps that is it."

depression, death and the self

"All the world's a stage, and all the men and women merely players: they have their exits and their entrances; and one man in his time plays many parts, his acts being seven ages."

William Shakespeare

Many people believe that death 'is it', a threshold to a realm of nothingness beyond which both our being and consciousness are annihilated and cease to be. Part of the *fear* of experiencing what 'no-thing-ness' is, is its association with *death* understood and anticipated in this way as a realm of absolute *nothingness* or as a non-being void of consciousness. Even people with this view of death however, are prepared to accept the common idea that the *process* of dying culminates in the unfoldment of a type of panoramic vision of our entire life in all its stages, as if viewing it as a play or drama unfolding on a stage – and as a sequence of all the situations we have been in, all the events we have experienced, all the people we have interacted with – and all the roles or parts we have acted or identified with. The retrospective unfoldment of the 'life panorama' as the vision of the entire life *drama* is like a parade of all those many different 'part selves' or 'part identities' that we were not fully aware of whilst living – precisely because we were so busily engaged in identifying *with* them and acting them as life roles or parts. Yet given the multiplicity of roles and part, selves or identities – actual or potential – that make up each individual a fundamental question arises. The question is this – what or who is the 'self' capable of becoming *aware* of our life-drama in all its stage and with it of all the parts we have taken – all our *dramatis personae* – yet doing so from a position 'off-stage' and independent of that parade of multiple identities, selves or personae? When we watch a play we can identify with any of the different characters portrayed and in this way perceive the entire drama from each of their quite different perspectives. A part, well-acted, allows us, even whilst being off-stage, to look out upon the stage itself through the very different eyes of each and every character that stands before us on it. Yet the awareness that enables us to so identify with each and every character on stage, cannot by definition, be reduced to the property of any one such character. Similarly, neither can the *awareness* of our lives as a panoramically unfolding drama – one involving the interplay of many different personalities and sub-personalities, parts and identities – be reduced to the property of any of these 'selves'. Indeed we can argue that, – in principle – the *awareness* of any self or set of selves cannot itself be reduced to the property of any self or selves, of any experienced identity. Instead the *awareness* of any self or identity *transcends* that self or identity.

on the ultimate meaning of depression

"Death is not my process, even if I belong to it. It belongs to the one who grants us life.

"Death is my constant shadow, is stranger than I am. Or is it HE himself, the God who experiments with himself as a man, in another life form?"

"In the hospital world ... I sit on the bed and write music that has nothing to do with the world of that last station [death]. The surroundings force me, as always, to force my way down within me, in order to reach the roots of my life. It is just that, the fact that something in me preserves its integrity, does not let itself be destroyed, that fills me with wonder, as before a miracle."

Swedish composer Allan Pettersson

Like language, awareness as such is no 'thing', but that which alone makes it possible for us to be aware or conscious of anything and everything. The only 'self' capable of being aware of our many selves and identities is not some self *with* a particular identity and awareness all of its own, but can only be a self with no particular nature or awareness of its own, a self that is *nothing* except *awareness as such* – not my awareness or yours but an awareness that is not the private property of any self or being. That self, which is nothing *but* awareness, is no 'thing' and yet it is not 'nothing'. It is not any particular self and yet it is no mere absence of self or 'no-self' – for it is an awareness of every possible self we can be or have been. It is no 'being' and yet it is no mere void of 'non-being'. It can neither die nor be born – and thus can have no fear of either birth or death. The Japanese sage Bankei called it our eternally *unborn* nature. As pure awareness, the unborn is that from all that was, is and can be is born. It is both no-thing and everything. It is both an absolute emptiness – as distinct from all its contents as space is distinct from all the objects within it – and an absolute *fullness*. For like space it also *embraces* everything within it. It is 'no-body' and yet it is not 'nobody'. For neither life nor consciousness begin with just *being* a body or mind, but rather with an *awareness* of being and an *awareness* of body and mind. It is towards *being* this singular awareness, one that is no-thing and no-body and yet all things and all bodies, that I believe the 'depressive process' is designed to lead us – allowing us to discover that 'God' which is no-one and every-one, no-being and all beings, no-self and yet the essence of self. In this sense the ultimate meaning of 'depression' does not lie in some psychological state – but in the ultimate reality that is awareness.

from the word to awareness

Through circling any element of our experience and turning it into what we think of as a clearly separable and identifiable 'thing' we do nothing but circumscribe and limit a larger and deeper *awareness* of that thing – and of other things. This does not mean that words do not or cannot speak *truly* – that they cannot speak *for* us truly, speak *to* us truly and 'speak us' truly. Words of this sort however – like those of a great seer, poet or thinker – arise not as names or denotations of things, but rather from depths and breadths of awareness transcending all things. They do not name things but name and in turn evoke a new *awareness*. It is this that enables such words to 'speak to us' – to take our awareness beyond – or deeper within – the narrow 'circles' of their conventionally accepted meanings.

Even so, we cannot *circumscribe* the world in words. That would be like trying to cover a blank white page with circles without leaving any gaps or empty spaces between them – whereas in reality it is that blank page and its empty spaces – not only those around but also those within all the circles we draw on – that is the very condition for drawing them in the first place. Awareness, like a blank page, is that which first makes space for the circles we draw in words. So let us not let these circles, and those who believe in the 'things' they circumscribe, run rings round us – but instead allow ourselves to feel embraced by the singular awareness that embraces and fills them all. For as the great 10th century Indian sage Abhinavagupta recognised: *"The being of all things that are recognised in awareness in turn depends on awareness."*

the depressive process

"To me it seems more and more as though our customary consciousness lives on the tip of a pyramid whose base within us (and in a certain way beneath us) widens out so fully that the farther we find ourselves able to descend into it, the more generally we appear to be merged into those things that, independent of time and space, are given in our earthly, in the widest sense, worldly existence."

Rainer Maria Rilke

The 'depressive process' is essentially a natural direction and movement of *awareness* – one in which we are drawn back down into ourselves – and ultimately also beyond ourselves. The awareness itself is nothing purely mental but a feeling awareness, in particular of the different ways in which we sense the inwardly felt spaces, tones and textures of our own body. In letting that awareness so descend, under the external pressure or internal weight of whatever problems we experience, we are also responding to the gravitational pull of our own spiritual and physical 'core' – our centre of gravity in all senses of that word. This core – the "depressive position" – is an inexhaustible inwardness that some feel as a bottomless and threateningly dark black whole. And yet like the type of black hole described in cosmology, going through it takes us ultimately out of and beyond ourselves into a larger awareness. Identifying with this awareness overcomes all sense of self-centredness, allowing us instead to feel the core of our being as a centre, not just of our personal self, but of that larger, trans-personal awareness itself – an awareness free of self-preoccupation, spacious enough to fully take in and respond to other people and the world around us, and one that widens rather than contracts the circles of awareness we previously inhabited. This widening of awareness is important, because in the simplest of terms, what we call 'depression' has to do with lack of awareness – not so much of things that are there in our lives but of things that are *absent*.

Depressive states are states in which we are *pregnant* with this still unborn awareness of absent or missing dimensions of our lives. Understanding this makes nonsense of the whole idea of 'treating', 'managing', 'fighting' or beating 'depression' – which makes no more sense than the idea of managing, fighting or beating a state of pregnancy.

Awareness, Abuse and 'Object Relations'

Abstract: towards a broader epistemology, sociology, semiology and symptomology of abuse-associated 'psychotic' structures and so-called 'borderline personality disorders'; integrating Kleinian, Lacanian and Marxist understandings of 'object relations' and object (ab-)use through the notion of the 'bad subject; presenting a neo-tantric philosophy of 'mind' or 'subjectivity' as a field of pure awareness or subjectivity ('The Awareness Principle') and suggesting a new awareness-based and body-oriented form of psychoanalytic 'mentalisation' theories and treatment approaches – 'Mentalising through the Body'.

Introduction

We cannot underestimate how frightening the world must feel for paranoid individuals who transform even the most harmless of words or events into persecutory attacks and the most harmless and well-intentioned of people into monstrous 'bad objects' and 'bad subjects' – reacting to and treating them accordingly. The problem is that even the most marginal awareness of doing so will be accompanied by or arouse a deep sense of guilt, and, along with this – a fear of retaliation that leaves them feeling even *more* open to attack, thus intensifying both their persecutory anxiety and paranoid hostility towards others – a hostility they are impelled to either take out on others or turn in on themselves, for example through self-harm, somatic symptoms or attacks of one form or another, or persecutory voices. Whatever the specificity or idiosyncrasies of their symptoms and behaviours, such individuals will be thus permanently trapped in a *fight-flight* state with long-term effects on both their body and on all their human relationships – forcing them to permanently seek out occasions to fight others and/or flee from them, or else retreating into even greater isolation (whether self-imposed or the result of illnesses or medications) from the human beings around them. For whosoever they are, 'good reasons' will be found for turning others into malign agents or 'bad subjects'. This said, nor can we reduce the paranoid pathology described above to a diagnostically labelled 'condition' or 'disorder' of a small group of aberrant individuals – for this is a pathology that underlies our entire war-torn world. In this article I will argue that it has its ultimate roots, not in individual instances of abuse, but in an all-pervasive mind-set which pictures 'consciousness' as mere relation of separate subjects and objects, and in doing so shapes our ways of being in the world and relating to others in its image.

A person, child or adult is 'abused' – whether economically or emotionally, psychologically, physically – or psychiatrically. That is to say they are handled, seen, treated – *used* – as if they were an *object*. Today much is made of the fact that 'child abuse' is far more common and widespread than previously thought. And yet this is thought of as something 'new', despite the fact that human history is replete with the mass abuse of men, women and children – and that on scales that make today's horrors pale. What remains *unthought* is the essential nature and reason for such abuse, above all its roots in ordinary object use and in that mode of consciousness associated with the 'subject-object' relation – a mode of consciousness we still take as 'normal', and a way of understanding it that we still take for granted as true.

'Consciousness' and 'cognition' have for long been falsely misunderstood, at least in the West, as a relation of separate 'subjects' and 'objects' – seen either as the *property* of an individual person as 'subject' or the *function* of a thing-like object such as the brain. Consciousness is seen as consciousness 'of' something – what Husserl called its 'intentional object'. Similarly, thoughts and emotions are understood as thoughts 'about' or emotions 'towards' something or someone, some subject or object. Consciousness and thought itself is also associated with the active *use* of objects, whether as means of production or as weapons. Yet what if object *use* – based on the reduction of consciousness to the relation of an active subject to a passive object – is the unthought essence and origin of all 'abuse'? For to say that person – whether child or adult, man or woman or child – is 'abused', is essentially to say that they are or have been handled, treated, seen – *used* – as if they were an object. Possible consequences of such (ab-)use can be:

1. The sense of being an active *subject* rather than a passive object of use is associated solely with the   abuser.
2. As a result, the abused person's basic sense of being a 'subject' or 'self' is eradicated – or rather *dis-located* to another. Their fundamental sense is: "I am not a self or active subject – only this other."
3. The person can only feel themselves to be a subject through (a) what Lacan called 'imaginary identifications' – identifications with *images* of themselves or others (b) seeing or seeking in others nothing but someone they can use as a 'self-object', one whose sole function is to offer a self-image or mirror for imaginary identifications, or (c) identifying with the abusing other and relating to others as objects in the same abusive manner as they were related to. In all cases the other is reduced to a mere *object* of action, perception, thought and emotion.
4. Interpersonal encounter in all situations thus becomes solely a medium of *object use*, rather than an opportunity for the individual to be 'taken out of themselves' through entering and experiencing the *subjective* world of another person.

The basis of what I term 'The Awareness Principle' is that there is a world of difference between, on the one hand, being subjectively *aware* of one's body and self, being *aware* of a thing or person, being *aware* of a thought or feeling, and, on the other hand, turning a thing or person into an *object* of thought or feeling – and thus also a potential object of *use* - including misuse or abuse. Diagram 1 below represents the nature of 'consciousness' understood as a relation of subject and objects in which different elements of our experience are intellectually or emotionally objectified. The ego is shown as a 'Subject' (S) standing above and apart from these elements of experience (shown as circular 'O's) that it looks down on as Objects:

Diagram 1

Awareness as punctiform subject (S) standing over and apart from its Objects (O):

Subject

S

O O O O O O O O O O OOOOO

[Objects]

In contrast, Diagram 2 represents such Objects not *as* objects but simply as any *elements of our experience* – whether in the form of events or people, things or thoughts, feelings or sensations. Pure subjective *awareness* of such elements of our experience, however, is not dependent on a pre-existing ego or *subject* standing over and apart from these elements, distancing itself from them, focusing on and objectifying them. For unlike this objectifying 'consciousness', awareness has the essential character of a space or 'field' surrounding and embracing every element of our experience – in the same way that space surrounds and embraces every 'thing' within it.

Diagram 2

Pure awareness or 'subjectivity' as a spacious field (the space within the larger circle) in which all apparent 'objects' (O) are embraced as elements of *subjective* experience, inner or outer.

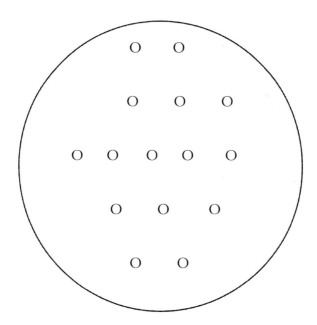

Throughout contemporary psychology, phenomenology and philosophy however, 'consciousness' or 'subjectivity' is still seen in the unquestioned and traditional way as the property or intentional activity of an isolated 'subject' or 'ego'– one separate from others and standing over and apart from its objects. 'Consciousness' is seen as something enclosed, as within a bubble, by the boundaries of the physical body, through which 'the subject' peers out at the world through "the peepholes of the senses".

Yet in many circumstances of violence, political persecution, torture, sexual abuse or economic exploitation and deprivation, even this narrow 'egoic' sense of subjectivity – of being an active, perceiving subject – is undermined by the experience of being perceived, handled and used as a mere object – the essence of 'abuse'. If, as a result however, the (ab-)used person's subjectivity is suppressed, dis-located to or even identified with the *abusing subject*, then further severe consequences result:

5. In order to sustain or revive even the restricted egoic sense of being a 'subject' it becomes a life necessity (and not just a normal *part* of life) to treat all things – including one's own body, one's own thoughts and feelings, and other people – as objects of use. This use includes everyday object use – which can become compulsive or obsessional (not least through the 'work ethic') and/or physical and emotional abuse of self or other.

6. The existential need to turn everything into an object of action, emotion or intellection means that any experience of *not* having an object for one's feelings – above all feelings of anger and rage – therefore becomes intolerable, a threat to one's very life or existence. Since an object for such 'bad feelings' must be found at all costs, whether in the form of a thing or person, the lack of such an object turns the feelings themselves into 'bad objects'. Projected outwardly, the bad objects may be perceived in the form of hallucinatory or dream images and/or actual physical objects. Alternatively they may take the form of somatic symptoms, or be felt within different body parts as uncomfortable sensations. These in turn may be explained as the work of malign alien spirits or – in modern medical terms – of

those 'foreign bodies' (toxins, cancer cells, viruses etc) that modern medicine claims to be the 'cause' of illness.

7. Since feeling any other *person* as an active and independent subject re-arouses the sense of being a mere passive object, the abused individual lacks experience of either their own body or of language as a medium of genuine *intersubjectivity*, which is instead experienced in a paranoid manner. By this I mean that both people and things are not experienced in their true subjectivity – as consciousnesses or subjectivities in their own right – but rather as agents, embodiments or materialisations of the original, malign and abusing subject. All things and people, subject and objects – become 'bad objects' (Klein), seen as symbolizing or serving the original 'bad subject'.

8. Subjective, feeling *awareness* of one's own body as a whole, and with it, a bodily feeling *awareness* of one's self as a whole – is replaced by identification with images, by the use of another solely as a mirroring external 'self-object' for such imaginary identifications, or simply by identifying bodily self-awareness with passive bodily suffering as such.

9. Suffering and associated *symptoms* can thus become not only a substitute or symbol but the *sole anchor* for the individual's bodily awareness and sense of self.

10. Any prolonged absence of suffering therefore, whether in the form of temporary alleviation of symptoms or positive pleasure – becomes intrinsically threatening – for since suffering and symptoms are the sole anchor for the individual's bodily sense of self, the loss of suffering or 'cure' of symptoms is tantamount to total *dissociation* from or death of self and body. It was one of Lacan's key psychoanalytic insights that the patient or 'analysand' does not actually wish to be 'cured' but rather needs his or her

suffering and symptoms, being still dependent on them for a sense of sensual aliveness or 'jouissance'.

Just as most forms of spiritual teaching aim at the overcoming of suffering however, so do most forms of medicine and psychiatry aim at 'curing' symptoms. Similarly, most forms of cognitive therapy, as well as New Age or 'Neuro-Linguistic' forms of 'positive thinking' encourage the use of the individual's ego ('the subject') to dispel and manipulate away any 'bad' or 'negative' feelings – thus implicitly treating them as 'bad objects'. Such forms of medical and psychological treatment or 'therapy' are thus themselves based on an essentially paranoid stance – turning bad feelings into bad objects and seeking to annihilate them. In this way however, they therefore affirm and reinforce the basic model of consciousness and psychic *structure* that underlies 'psychosis', understood not primarily as a mere psychiatric grouping of diagnostic symptoms but as an underlying psychic *structure*. In Klein's terms this structure is a 'paranoid-schizoid' relation to the world. The relation is 'schizoid' because the 'paranoid' side comes itself from a basic *splitting* of 'subject' and 'object – one that pervades not just *philosophies* of consciousness but we take as normal and 'healthy' consciousness as such – despite all the barbarity and abuse that 'mysteriously' arises in its midst.

We can express the general dynamics at work here abstractly through a number of emotional 'equations' or 'transformations'. For example the equation or transformation of a subjective awareness of 'feeling bad' to labelling certain feelings as bad, objectifying them as 'negative' or 'bad' feelings – and then identifying or equating these objectified bad feelings with a 'bad object' that is responsible for them, whether in the form of an everyday object, body part, virus, gene – or person. This creation of 'bad objects' is nothing unusual or exceptional. Take for example an author who is feeling 'bad' about (e.g. stuck or critical towards) a piece she is writing or has written. The 'feeling bad' towards the writing as object easily becomes a 'bad feeling' which is felt as an object in itself and then, in Klein's terms projectively identified with or 'into' the writing. The objective physical form of the writing – whether a finished text, a paper draft or a computer file, can then quite literally be felt as a 'bad object' – and as such is *physically* avoided until or unless a good feeling towards it returns. Similarly, a building or location associated with feeling bad may itself become a bad object, not simply by 'association' with the bad feeling but through its outward projection – as an object – into the objects making up the building or location – which is then itself felt as a 'bad object' and avoided.

Many types of physical objects once felt as good, can turn 'bad' – whether a type of food, a precious object gifted by an unfaithful partner, or a set of books whose subject or author is now perceived as 'bad'. These are simple everyday examples of paranoid responses to 'bad objects' created by transformative processes of projective identification. Nazi book burning was a typical example of objects perceived as expression of a 'bad subject' – the Jew. Conversely, the treatment of Wagner's music as a bad object merely through its misconceived and malodorous association with Nazism is a typical example of another transformation – what might be called the *displacement* of the bad subject. Listed below is an overall set of key transformations relating good and bad objects and subjects of the sort that can result extreme 'paranoid', 'psychotic' or 'borderline' behaviours:

1. *Feeling transformed into an object* by another as subject.
2. *Identifying others* with the original malign or 'bad' subject.
3. Seeking the 'good subject' through identification with *images*.
4. *Identifying with the bad subject* by (ab-)using others *as* objects.
5. *Using* others as 'self-objects' to mirror imaginary identifications.

6. Needing to turn every element of one's subjective experience *into an object*.
7. *Needing an object*, whether thing or person, for all thoughts and emotions.
8. Perceiving real or imagined objects as 'bad objects' – as *agents* of the bad subject.
9. Identifying with or inflicting *suffering* as the sole way of feeling and affirming oneself *as* a subject.

Then there is the primary 'object relations'* dynamic identified by Klein: alternation between loving and hating, being grateful to and spitefully envying anyone who embodies the good or 'whole object' – in essence a *good subject* – someone whose subjectivity or awareness is receptive and open rather than objectifying. Failure to 'internalise' or 'introject' the *good subject* – to embody it – transforms it, through *envy*, into a *bad object* and thus also the object of destructive attacks. These in turn rebound on the attacker, being essentially self-attacks, thus intensifying their distress and envy. Only if the individual can feel guilt and embody impulses towards reparation for these destructive attacks can they themselves begin to feel their own subjectivity as 'good'. Thus it is only through allowing feelings of guilt and gratitude that Klein saw a movement from the 'paranoid schizoid position' to a 'depressive position' being possible – a position in which the other is no longer split into a good and a bad object or subject and thus *alternatively* loved and hated, but instead seen, felt and related to as a 'whole object' capable of internalization/introjection. In the analytic process, this movement requires a corresponding transition from 'paranoid transference' (rage directed at the analyst for threatening the analysand's psychopathic defences) to 'depressive transference' (the analysand becoming aware of the depths of their own envy and hatred, and allowing themselves depressive feelings of guilt and shame).

The set of transformations outlined above *appears* to begin with mistreatment and abuse by an original malign subject in the form of a bad or 'evil' person. This is certainly how it is experienced. But what makes a person violent or malevolent, what makes them use or abuse another? Is it some inherited gene or intrinsic force of evil we can 'objectify'? Or is it ultimately the root identification – and experience – of 'consciousness' – as a subject-object relation, as the private property of a subject or 'I', or even as the very activity of objectification? If so, is there any other way of understanding and experiencing the nature of consciousness – one that would advance humankind beyond its past and present barbarity? Yes there is. It is the understanding and direct experience that 'consciousness', – understood as pure awareness – is *not* essentially a relation of subject and object, and is not the private property of individual subjects or the material function of any biological objects. To attain this understanding and experience of *awareness* is very difficult today – living as we do in a global capitalist economic culture which thrives precisely by turning people into things – into labour power to be bought and sold on the market, to be used and mercilessly exploited for profit or left uselessly on the shelf; all according to the whims of the market and its religion – the Monotheism of Money.

The more the mass media focus on such horrors as sexual abuse of children the more they conceal and detract awareness from the *economic, political and military* abuse of *adults* which is undoubtedly one of its key causes. That does not mean that we can blame all social ills on social-economic deprivation or 'the system'. Individuals are responsible for their actions, whatever their social circumstances – and there are actions that are right and wrong, and some – such as violence – that are unforgivable. What is certain is that no good comes from retributive violent punishment. Prison and death sentences are no more *forgivable* forms of violation and abuse than those they are used to punish.

So what of medical psychiatry – or else psychotherapy, counselling or New Age 'spirituality'? No good can come of these either so long as either victims or perpetrator are made to play different psychological games of objectification with their own experience or else have it chemically anaesthetised. What is needed is to advance them – and all human beings – to a higher *awareness* of their own experiencing in all its elements and thus to a new experience of the nature of awareness itself. Central to this advance is the recognition that *the awareness* of a thought or feeling, impulse or emotion, sensation or desire – however intense – is not itself a thought or feeling, impulse or emotion, sensation or desire, but is something essentially free of all such elements of our experience. Awareness alone embraces all such elements of our experience whilst remaining distinct from them all. It is such pure awareness that allows us to *freely choose* which elements of our experience to follow or identify with – and which not – whilst ensuring we do not lose ourselves in any element of our experience, or let it dictate our actions unawares. Awareness alone is what lets us refind this truly *free subjectivity* – but without any need to *objectify* ourselves or others.

Language and Lacan

Without the cultivation of awareness, supposedly normal or 'neurotic' consciousness – rooted in the objectified or objectifying 'subject' – is easily transformed into so-called 'psychosis'. What we take as 'normality' is in reality what Bollas[1] has called 'normosis' – normosis and psychosis being two sides of the same coin – the reduction of consciousness to a subject-object relation. Freud himself saw "no fundamental but only quantitative distinctions between normal and neurotic life." He applied psychoanalysis as a way of cultivating the patient's awareness in the treatment of 'normal' neurotic symptoms – 'normosis' – but did not see it as a feasible way of treating 'psychosis'. Melanie Klein, on the other hand, understood 'psychosis' not as a medical-diagnostic label for particular types of symptom but as an infantile 'paranoid-schizoid' mode of relating – one that remains more or less latent or active in *all* adults. In contrast, Lacan re-affirmed in new linguistic terms a basic distinction between neurotic and psychotic character structures and symptoms. Central to his perspective was his association of psychosis with a failure to fully enter the realm of *language* ('the symbolic') as opposed to the realm of lived experience, suffering or 'jouissance' on the one hand, and a world of imaginary identifications on the other.

Like awareness, language is no 'thing'. For though it finds expression in the 'objective' form of the spoken and written word, language *as such* is not itself any 'object'. Nor do words themselves, as 'signifiers' merely denote or represent specific objects or 'signifieds'. The meaning of language does not lie in referring to things but in 'deferring' meaning. Thus even in the most seemingly commonplace of everyday verbal interactions between people, and despite their apparent reference to everyday things and events, we can never pin down 'in' words what it is that people are *saying to* one another – as subjects – *through* their words, whatever these words seem to be referring to or 'about'. Even in just *referring* to and talking about ourselves we are effectively using this 'subject' word 'I' to *objectify* ourselves – thus forever *deferring* expression of our silent, *subjective* awareness of self.

Language automatically bars and defers direct expression of the self, subject or 'I' that is speaking – 'the speaking self' – because the spoken self or "I" is one that is spoken *about* and thus constantly *objectified* through language itself. It is because of this that the unspoken awareness or subjectivity of the individual is forced to seek expression in other ways – not through what they say about themselves, 'in' words but through what the words they choose say about them. For as Freud well recognised, our every choice of words *can say more* about *us* than we intend or mean to say through it.

In Lacan's linguistic reinterpretation of and 'return' to Freud, it is through language – something that is not our private property but something shared with others – that we are prevented from directly expressing ourselves, but bound, as if by an iron law, to *constantly construct* and reconstruct our sense of self or subjectivity through our very acts of speech. In the very act of speaking about ourselves using the words that are all shared social constructs, we deny direct expression to the private self that is doing the speaking.

The 'law' of language is that it *speaks us* as much if not more than we speak it – that it *defers* expression of subjective experience in the very act of *referring* to it – transforming into a linguistic construct the very 'subject' that seeks to express itself through language, and transforming subjective experiences into linguistic objects. Yet it is precisely this law, according to Lacan, which is anathema for the psychotic. For the latter wants not only to *know* themselves to be a subject, and to know who they are as a subject – but to be able to grasp this 'gnosis' or self-knowledge, pin it down, express it and penetrate others with it *using* language as a tool. The fact that this is impossible – that language cannot be *used* for this subjective purpose is something the psychotic cannot face – for it means coming face to face with the reality that language as such – and not any individual subject – is itself the ultimate objectifying power, and thus, for the psychotic the equivalent to the 'bad subject' writ large. The problem however, is that since language is something shared, it is not and can never be the *property* or purely *private* tool of any individual subject, good or bad.

For Lacan there is and can be no such thing as a 'borderline' condition or disorder hovering somewhere between neurotic and psychotic symptomologies and psychic structures. Instead what defines the psychotic in contrast to the neurotic is their inability to tolerate the gap or abyss that language opens up between direct subjective experience and its objectifying expression – someone, therefore, whose whole relation to language or 'the symbolic order' is 'foreclosed'. As a result they can only relate to it in a fantastic way – *as if* it *were* an independent subject in its own right (for example 'The Word' as the person of 'Christ') or else the *voice* of an imaginary subject (for example the voice of Yahweh addressing Abraham). Hence the paradox that those who 'hear voices', human or divine, can rarely say much or anything about *who* is speaking – and yet it is of the utmost importance to them to hear the words spoken to them as the voice of some specific subject or 'who'. This type of hearing is essentially the expression of a specific type of psychotic *deafness* – a deafness to the many ways in which words themselves and language as such can speak to us, touch our feelings, open us to new concepts, indeed lend us new ears and a new voice – yet *without* their needing to be any specific subject or speaker or 'who' behind them.

"Listen not to *me* but to The Logos" Heraclitus

"Language speaks"…"Listen to Language" Martin Heidegger

"The unconscious is the Speech of the Other." Lacan

A key *symptom* of psychotic structures is that the tangible, tactile body of another person ('The Flesh') is seen as a mere specular object – a fixed or changing *image*. In contrast the speech or 'Word' of another (spoken or read) is experienced as meaningful *only* through the manner in which it 'becomes Flesh'. Its 'meaning' for the psychotic hearer lies not in the awareness it communicates or its conceptual content but *solely* in the way in which it is felt as an object (good or bad) in a tangible, fleshly way – for example through the way it emotionally affects the hearer's body or induces immediate emotional or bodily sensations of pleasure or pain ('jouissance').

Another symptom is unawareness of the meaning of words and events, speech and behavioural acts and events *for others*. The psychotic's world of meaning necessarily centres entirely and exclusively around themselves. For it to be otherwise would be to admit the existence of 'other minds' or 'other subjects'. This is something very difficult or painful for the psychotic since all other subjects are tainted by association or identification with the 'bad subject' – and thus with annihilation of one's own subjectivity. Inter-subjective empathy or resonance is thus ruled out from the start. Being alone, the psychotic suffers isolation. Being with others, he or she is charged with paranoid anxiety. What Winnicott recognised as a fundamental condition of psychic health – the capacity to "be alone with others" – to feel oneself more strongly in and through the bodily co-presence of another – is therefore ruled out or 'foreclosed' from the start.

A third, well-recognised but not fully understood symptom of psychosis is *gaze avoidance*. The psychotic can perceive and even 'read' the face and eyes of another but not *receive* their gaze. For receiving the gaze of the other – however benign or loving its subjective quality – means potentially opening oneself to the objectifying gaze of the bad subject.

A fourth symptom is a constant and persistent search for reasons, however trivial to turn a good feeling, good object or good subject into something bad.

A fifth symptom is blocked communication or speech acts. For all communication is tinged with unbearable ambivalence towards the other in the form of love and hate, gratitude and envy, seeking and avoiding contact with other subjects. It is this ambivalence that, in the paranoid-schizoid position, is felt as unbearable anxiety and bad object in itself – hence Klein's association of the depressive position with the capacity to contain ambivalent feelings towards others rather than splitting the other, splitting self and other – and thereby also splitting the self – thus creating a polarized world of good and bad objects, or of good and 'evil' subjects.

A sixth and major symptoms is the one that makes 'psychoses' and what is now termed 'borderline personality disorder' difficult to treat *through* analysis or any form of therapeutic talking cure. This symptom expresses itself in the way that even the most well-intended and carefully worded analytic insights and interpretation are not received as helpful modes of self-understanding or thoughtful words by the analysand – indeed they are not even taken in as words or thoughts at all but rather felt as bad objects to be blocked or hurled back.

For all of us there are truths which may indeed be extremely painful to accept and face. For the personality dominated by psychotic structures and transformation, the very articulation of these painful truths by another is perceived as a *pernicious and painful attack by the other* – one that must be met by defensive and destructive counter-attacks which focus on everything but the actual thought-content and truth-value of the word. Here Lacan's formulation – "The unconscious is the speech of the other" – takes on a specifically Kleinian dimension of meaning by association with her analyses of primitive defences and persecutory anxieties. At the same time, Klein's analysis of paranoid-schizoid defences lends itself to interpretation within Lacan's strict definition of psychosis as a psychical structure in which 'the paternal metaphor' – language as a third element in the mother-child dyad is *foreclosed* – both as a medium of inter-subjectivity and as a way by which the individual can begin to healthily construct or re-construct a positive sense of autonomous subjectivity.

According to Lacan, a psychotic structure manifests as psychotic breakdowns and psychotic symptoms not through an inevitable, internal process but through some form of *external* confrontation with 'the paternal metaphor' – the father being not only any real or imaginary male but also 'the symbolic father'. The symbolic father is essentially the 'symbolic order' as such. This is the role of language in constituting and defining the self *as* a subject in the very act of speaking about it. Through unaware identification with the spoken subject pronoun 'I' and the words or 'predicates' we attach to it, we 'subject' ourselves to language in the very act of objectifying ourselves through it. Unawareness of language means deluding ourselves that the self we are speaking about using the subject word 'I' (the *signifying* or *spoken* self) merely 'expresses', 'denotes', 'describes' or 'refers' a pre-linguistic self that is doing the speaking (the *signified* or *speaking* self). In reality, the signified or spoken self constantly shapes and reshapes our experience of the speaking or signified self. Yet *submitting* ourselves to the way in which language is necessarily 'castrating' – *subjecting* us to its power through the way we are bound to *objectify* ourselves through it – it is also a necessary aspect of socialisation, a surrender of fixed ego identifications to the social realm of language ('the symbolic order') that Lacan associates with the paternal element of the Oedipal triad ('the paternal metaphor').

Whilst the term 'object' is central in Kleinian thought and 'object relations' theory, in Lacanian theory the term 'signifier' takes the place of the 'object'. The complete absence or 'foreclosure' of the paternal function which defines 'psychosis' for Lacan is the absence of a central object, signifier or *signifying object* necessary for the constitution of the individual's subjectivity through speech. A key difference between Klein and Lacan however, is that whereas for the former the central, most significant 'object' and therefore also the locus of object-loss is the *mother*, for Lacan what is central is the phallus – not as penis but as a general symbol or signifier of *absence* and thus the desire of the mother. The child assumes that it should fill the *lack* that defines the mother's desire – and all desire – by *becoming the phallus*. By 'phallus' then, is not meant the penis, nor any 'phallic symbol' thereof. Instead Lacan understands 'phallic symbolism' in a quite different way – as 'the symbolic phallus' and a symbolic *function*. This function is not to serve as symbolic object *of* desire but rather as a *signifier* of 'desire' – desire itself being understood not as something with a definite object or 'signified' that can fulfil it, but rather as a lack that can never be objectified or fulfilled. This is where Lacan's novel triadic distinction between *need, desire and demand* is of fundamental significance.

Whereas needs have an object that can fulfil them, and can be articulated in language as requests, desire as such has an absolute character of a 'demand' for unconditional love that can never be fulfilled through need-satisfaction. 'Desire' is the indeterminate (object-less) and therefore unfulfilable 'leftover' from need-satisfaction, thus transforming need-satisfaction itself into a potential source of frustration – the frustration of that *desire* which cannot be met by any object of need, provided or withheld, attainable or unattainable. The infantile intensification of *demands* for need satisfaction from the mother – or any other – is an expression of this frustrating gap between needs and their fulfilment on the one hand, and desire on the other.

This *leftover* or *lack* at the heart of desire also corresponds, in Lacan's terms, to the unavoidable *gap* between language – 'the signifier' – and anything we seek to signify or symbolise through it. The phallus is thus not only signifier of desire but a *signifier of all signifiers* – all of which open up a gap between signifier and the signified which has the fundamental character of desire, understood as an unfulfilable lack.

In Lacan's interpretation of Freud then, the lack at the heart of the mother's desire is not the real father and his penis, but the phallus as signifier of lack and the 'paternal function'. For the child, the paternal function is the role of the father's word – and of language as such – in the socialisation process through which the child is led beyond its primal dyadic bond with the mother and into the larger world of social communication with its cultural signs and symbols. A significant implication of this understanding is that the essence of any 'talking cure' lies precisely in *not* being reducible to its apparent professional medium – a purely one-to-one or *dyadic* interaction between an analyst, therapist or counsellor and their analysand or client. On the contrary, in the framework of Lacanian psychoanalytic practice, it is of fundamental significance for the analyst *not* to serve as substitute for the hitherto absent 'good mother' but rather to *triangulate* – to embody the missing 'third' element in the primordial dyad. This 'third' can be understood as awareness *as such*, understood as a field transcending and embracing both parties of the dyad. Alternately, in Lacan's terms, the third is the 'paternal function' of language as such as a trans-individual Other – not to be confused with a personal other in the dyad. The 'paternal function' of language as this Third or Other is to insert a wedge into the dyad. Only in this way is a space opened for the individual to experience a sense of subjective autonomy independent of the dyad, and to *give* their Desire reality through language and the naming word – 'The Name of the Father' – even whilst accepting that it will forever elude full expression in speech.

Margaret Mahler's analysis of mother-child 'symbiosis' and 'separation-individuation' processes in childhood allows us to link Lacan's model of analytic triangulation with Lawrence Hedge's analysis[2] of psychic defences used specifically by the 'borderline personality' to *prevent* intrusion by a Third or Other into the dyad. He calls these defences 'scenarios' and defines them as any form of "interpersonal exchanges which the patient arranges, manipulates or insists upon setting up with the therapist and/or other persons" in order to either replicate or elaborate early experiences. That these scenarios are all created and enacted through one-to-one exchanges is central to their essential purpose – which is to protect or perpetuate a purely *dyadic* relationship to another in whatever way possible, whether through aggression or pacification, speech or silence, or even by destructive attacks on the dyad as such. For even breaking a dyadic relation is itself a relational act that confirms the dyad *as* a dyad. On the basis of Mahler's concept of child-mother symbiosis, Lawrence relates the need to create such scenarios as an expression of a *symbiotic yearning* for a type of deep inner connection or symbiotic unity with another of a sort that was either *never* experienced, whether in childhood or adulthood, or whose *loss* the individual cannot tolerate. Being something that can *never* be met by another as a mere object of the individual's need and demands, 'symbiotic yearning' is wholly analogous to Lacan's concept of 'desire'. It is what demands the manipulative creation of e 'scenarios' designed to protect the dyad as sole *potential* space for fulfilment of the desire for symbiotic and sexual union – as universally symbolised by the womb or vagina (Yoni) and the phallus (Lingam).

That Lacan's own understanding of 'phallic symbolism' is no mere theoretic idiosyncrasy belonging to Lacan's interpretation of Freud is shown by its function as an ancient and universal signifying object in both cultural and religious symbolism. As a tantric religious symbol the phallus or *lingam* (Skt) may take the shape of a penis, yet it can equally be a mere shapeless stone. Indeed the root meaning of the word Lingam, even though it 'refers' to the phallus as penis – is nothing *but* 'mark or symbol'. Its variable, abstract or relatively formless forms serve its principal religious function – to be a symbol of the *symbolic nature of all things* – which reveal the manifest presence of a God (the divine masculine) only symbolically – in its absence – yet do so precisely through its manifestation as *signifying objects* (the divine feminine or mother) in any shape or form. In tantra too, *erotic desire* is affirmed rather than negated as a fundamental aspect of the divine, the 'ascetic' dimension of tantric practice having to do more with the renunciation of need gratification through objects. Its aim is the supreme bliss of an experienced unity between the divine masculine and divine feminine attained through ceasing to experience the latter in any way at all as a realm of *objects*, but rather as the creative power (Shakti) of the divine-masculine experienced as pure subjectivity or awareness (Shiva). Hence the definition of Shiva as the 'erotic ascetic'. Hence also the tantric iconography of the divine-feminine as destroyer of the world *as a realm of objects* – with the goddess Kali portrayed as wearing a garland of skulls (signifying the empty egoic subject) and a waist belt of cut off male hands signifying the ego's constant *grasping* for intellectual, emotional or sexual satisfaction in the form of an object. Yet since in tantra things are as much *symbols* as words are, what Lacan calls the Symbolic is associated primarily with the divine feminine (Shakti) rather than the divine masculine – except that the 'symbol' or 'signifier' is taken here in its sensuously tangible sense – not simply as 'the Word' but as that primordial vibration ('Spanda'), sound ('OM') and alphabet of primordial sounds (Matrika), which is the mantric mother or 'matrix' of all sensory, biological, psychical and material *structures*. Shakti, as the divine feminine, is the innate *linguistically* of all that is – every thing and word that exists being a linguistic expression, embodiment or materialisation of a set of primordial sounds or phonemes.

In this context it is also interesting to note that whilst in Lacan's neo-Freudian psychoanalytic terminology the power of language in destroying ego identifications is understood as 'castrating' it is understood quite differently in the tantric tradition – where it is named and experienced not as castration but as ultimate *bliss* (Ananda) and *liberation* (Moksha) through the *infinite spaciousness and power of pure awareness* – liberation not only from ego-identifications and the limited and delusory ego or 'subject' but *also* from the limiting nature of language and of ordinary object-focussed consciousness. And in contrast to the Western fetishism of the phallus as male sexual organ, the tantric tradition identifies the divine-masculine as Lingam with the body as a whole – and indeed with all bodies and the entire "embodied cosmos" – the latter being at the same time a containing vessel or vagina (*yoni*) for the power of awareness that is the divine feminine.

In tantra, the Divine – like language, and like awareness or subjectivity as such – is that which both constitutes all objects and yet is no objectifiable thing, being or subject in itself. Instead it is *signified* by things, as by the word. Thus in the Indian tradition, crude worship or 'idolatry' of the word or 'graven image' is understood as quite distinct from true religious feeling – which can arise only through revering the divine 'flavour' (Rasa) of the awareness or 'spirit' which religious words, idols and icons manifest and transmit. (In this context it is interesting to note that Lacan's own idiosyncratic style of discourse, in both his seminars and analytic practices was itself influenced by the Rasa linguistics of the 10th century tantric adept Abhinavagupta, which emphasized the non-objectifying but rather subjectively *suggestive* power of the word and speech.)

Lacan's psychoanalytic understanding of the symbolic function of the phallus also bears a very specific relation to tantric understandings of sexuality and gender difference. From a Lacanian perspective, the psychoanalytic essence of gender lies in the *symbolic* difference between *having* a phallus in the form of a penis (male) or in not having a penis and *being* the phallus (female). This corresponds to the tantric distinction between the divine masculine as 'power holder' and the divine feminine, which is identified with power as such. In terms of the tantric tradition 'being the phallus' therefore, does not means 'having' or 'holding' its power – equivalent to 'having a penis'. Instead it means allowing one's body as a whole – and not some specific organ – to be pervaded by the vital power that is the divine feminine or 'Shakti' (a word whose root meaning *is* power).

In contrast, within the Freudian-Lacanian psychoanalytic framework, the phrase 'being the phallus' has a quite different connotation – seeking to fulfil the imagined desire of the mother. The essence of the Oedipal challenge for Lacan lies precisely in no longer seeking to be the phallus – to fill the lack or hole behind her imagined desire through identification with imaginary self-images. Hence the role of the 'paternal function' in breaking the child's search for identity through imaginary and ideal identifications by means of the 'name', 'word' or 'law' of the father, thus going beyond the realm of the 'Imaginary Order' and entering the Symbolic Order – the realm of language. For this is a realm in which identity constantly eludes fixation as something merely signified by words or signifiers but instead is forever constituted and re-constituted by signifying acts – acts of speech.

For the heterosexual male, the abandonment of imaginary identifications – 'being the phallus' – is felt as castration and opposed through defiance of the *word* of the father. Using as an example Freud's analysis of the case of Dora, Lacan contrasts this mode of defiance with that of the homosexual female who defies the *desire* of the father. "You want me to love men. You will have as many dreams about love of men as you wish." In other words "In your dreams!" Lacan defined this as "defiance in the form of derision".

"If you re-read the case [Freud's case of Dora] you will see the obviously provocative role of this girl who, dogging the footsteps of some *demi-mondaine* whom she had found in the town, constantly made show of the chivalrous attentions she paid the girl until one day, meeting her father – what she meets in her father's gaze in unconcern, disregard, contempt for what is happening in front of him – she immediately throws herself over the railing of a local railway bridge. Literally, she can no longer conceive, other than by destroying herself, of the function she had, that of showing the father how one is, oneself, an abstract, heroic, unique phallus ..."
Lacan

It is in seeking to sexually embody the position of being the phallus for another woman – or being the woman that desires it – that the homosexual female *defies the desire of the real or symbolic father.* The desire of the father is simply the desire of *man as such* – which according to Lacan is not in essence a desire for a sexual object but rather, as Kojeve saw it, a desire for "the desire of the Other".

"Desire is human only if the one desires, not the body, but the Desire of the other ... to be 'desired' or 'loved' in his human value ... In other words, all human, anthropogenetic Desire is, finally, a function of the desire for 'recognition'."

Kojeve, 1947

The question of recognition is 'Who am I for the other?' – not least the other who may be preoccupied with their own needs, and in relation to whom one may experience oneself as a mere instrument of use or object of demand for their gratification, and whose own desire is an indeterminate lack stemming from a sense of non-being and not a valuing of one's own being.

'Desire' as desire for the *desire* of the Other can in no way be fulfilled through demands or object use, let alone sexual need gratification in the form of forced sex or sexual abuse – however often repeated. The latter however, can be understood as creating trauma of the necessary intensity for the victim to completely 'foreclose' the 'paternal function', thus laying down the basic psychotic *structure* that may – or may not – come to expression in psychotic symptoms. This makes all the more interesting and significant Lacan's emphasis on the role of external encounters with the 'symbolic father' or 'paternal function' in triggering such symptoms in the context of histories of sexual abuse.

Lacan's whole neo-Freudian theoretics however, also sheds light on hidden dimensions of gender identity and their relation to the essential role of the 'symbolic father' and 'paternal function' in the Oedipal triad, being that which facilitates (a) separation of the child from identification with the desire of the mother ('being the phallus') and (b) separation from the entire realm of identifications (successful or failed) with *images* of oneself – whether one's own, those of the mother and her desire, or any others. It is separation through language ('the Symbolic') from the realm of 'the Imaginary' – identification with self-images – that is felt as catastrophic loss or 'castration' by both the male and female child. Yet it is this very separation or loss alone that enables the individual to feel their own authentic, non-imaginary and non-delusive subjective reality ('the Real').

In Wilfred Bion's neo-Kleinian 'theory of thinking' on the other hand, the basic experience of absence, lack or loss is related to early infant-mother relations rather than to the Oedipal triad, and can lead in two quite distinct directions – either to the substitution of the absent thing with *thought* (the signifying word) or to what Klein termed 'projective identification'[3]. Bion understood the latter as based on an inability to tolerate the frustration of lack or absence of an object and to *think* the object in its absence. Instead the very *absence* of an object (whether thing or person) is experienced *as* an object in itself – the 'bad object'. Instead of *thought* filling the mind

198

space of the absent object, the absence is transformed into a bad object and projected outwards into things or people. Frustration is relieved by 'evacuating' the bad object through such processes of projective identification – but only at the expense of ensuring its return in the form of persecutory anxiety or images which come back – in place of thought – to fill the now further evacuated and thus enlarged space or 'void' of absence. Similarly, in the thinking of both Freud and Heidegger, the fundamental character of 'anxiety' as *anxiety* – as opposed to *fear* – is the lack of a tangible or thinkable object or 'cause' for it. Conversely *any* sense of absence or lack can be experienced as anxiety – thus leading (in Kleinian terms) to the *projection* of an imagined persecutory object and with it the transformation of 'free-floating' anxiety into persecutory anxiety or 'panic attacks'.

In contrast to anxiety, I have written of *depressive* states as states that result from a fear of fully surrendering to what I call the depressive *process*. Surrendering to the depressive process means submitting to the gravitational pull of the 'void' or 'black hole' of non-being felt in depressive states – a gravitational pull whose function is a healthy one of drawing us so far 'down' into ourselves that we 'bottom out'. Only by letting ourselves feel so 'down' and go 'down' fully to a 'rock bottom' or 'zero-point' state can we ultimately 'find our feet' again – feeling able to once again stand firmly on the innermost, foundational *ground* of our being.

Whereas Bion identified anxiety with early pre-Oedipal infant-mother relations and with the absence of the object – embodied and symbolised by the breast and mother – Lacan completely reversed this classical object-relations view of anxiety as having to do with object loss and separation from the mother ('separation anxiety'). Instead he put forward the counter-concept of a type of primordial *non-separation anxiety* based on attachment to the mother and *bondage* to the primordial infant-mother *dyad*, unbroken by the Oedipal *triad*.

Within this perspective it is not the absence of the mother but her all-pervading and enveloping presence that fails to create a space of absence in which the baby can begin to experience its autonomous subjectivity and which can also serve as its own psychic womb or vacuum for the gestation of thought and speech – a place of entry into the Symbolic order symbolised by the father. Nevertheless Bion's insights into the psychical transformations involved in the birth of thinking – or its miscarriage and substitution by 'projective identification' – remain highly congruent with Lacan's understanding of psychosis as a repudiation and foreclosure of the 'paternal metaphor', whose lack or absence creates a psychical void which is then filled by delusory phantasies (or experienced as insatiable drives). Within both of these analytic frameworks private phantasy images or voices replace the social realm of language and thought as the locus of signification and meaning – and thus distort or preclude social relationships. In contrast, what might be called the 'spiritual therapeutics' of tantric *yoga* are based on meditative identification *with* the void and empty space – experienced not simply *as* an empty void but as a space of pure awareness that is fundamentally distinct *from* – and thus also quintessentially *free* from – *all* the contents or 'objects' of consciousness within it, 'good' or 'bad'. Pure awareness – 'The Awareness Principle' rather than Lacan's 'Language Principle' – is understood as the key to health as well as freedom and spiritual maturation.

The new relevance I believe that such *awareness-based* approaches to healing have lies in the fact that language is *no longer* the medium of mature socialisation that it used to be. For we are now living in an era of *social psychosis* totally dominated by the exploitation of imaginary or phantasy identifications as a source of profit. Our global capitalist and consumer culture is one in which language and thought have given way to the *image*, and in which subjective identity is marketed in the form of objects – of commodities that offer the satisfaction of attaining an ideal self-image through identification with a 'brand image'. The message is simple – you too can become the male image of a Beckham or female Beauty model by purchasing a related commodity branded with that image. This makes Lacan's distinction between the 'ideal ego' and the 'ego ideal' even more pertinent. For whereas the 'ideal ego' is an ideal self-image the individual seeks to assume, the 'ego ideal' is the subject in whose eyes this self-image is the 'ideal' one. The 'ideal ego' may also be associated with the 'ego ideal' in the form of a person. Yet there is a still more powerful 'ego ideal' – one which does not exist in the form of a specific person or subject but is instead represented by images idealized within an entire culture.

Within contemporary culture, the celebrity model or footballer is not an 'ego ideal' in the form of a real person but a mere image – the image of an 'ideal ego' which the individual then internalises as the 'ego ideal' or locus of perception from which to view and judge their own conformity to their ideal ego or self-image. Not surprising then that, as Richard Garner reports (2007) "'Primary schools have been engulfed by a wave of 'anti-social behaviour, materialism and the cult of celebrity', according to the most in-depth study for 40 years." The cult of celebrity explains also why the loss of a cultural 'ego ideal' in the form of a real person such as Elvis or Princess Di can be such a blow to the mass psyche. For if the person is dead, so also is the phantasy of a *personal* relationship to them as 'ego ideal' – either dampening or obsessively amplifying the *delusory identification*s with the 'ideal ego' that they provided an *image* of.

In pre-capitalist cultures it was 'God' or the monarch as God-King – understood as a supreme being or absolute subject – that represented the ultimate 'ego ideal', being the externally judging 'eye' or 'I' under whose constant gaze the individual felt themselves judged and whose written or oral 'law' the individual sought to live up to. Since the 'death of God' within secular capitalist culture, however, the individual has become paramount – albeit as subject whose individuality is offered only in the paradoxical form of standardized, mass produced and media-promoted self-images or 'ideal egos', themselves identified with mere *objects* in the form of commodities. Individuation is reduced to a competitive drive for private possession of idealized or 'aspirational' objects or lifestyles. This goes hand in hand with the continuing delusion that identity, individuality and consciousness itself are necessarily the *private property* of the individual subject, ego or 'I'. From a Marxist perspective, Lacan's emphasis on the dominance of the Signifier over the signified – the belief that language constitutes its own objects and indeed our own subjectivity – reflects the way in which language itself has taken the place of God in both philosophy and psychoanalysis.

Yet since language is a medium of communicative exchange of meanings, what Lacan's thinking really reflects is a social development parallel to the one identified by Marx as central to the development of capitalist economics – the subjugation of the concrete sensual properties and 'use value' of a commodity to its exchange value or market value, and the elevation of exchange value – signified by Money – to a monotheistic God whose whims are realized through the Holy Ghost of The Market. Unfortunately however, in capitalist culture such a thing as a great work of art or a profound philosophy has no 'use' and no 'use value' besides its exchange value – its market value. Worse still, the market places a premium on 'popular culture' – on a mass market which can only be made profitable through the superficialisation, standardization or dumbing-down of the cultural commodities offered through it. Indeed as Heidegger warned, any type of deep 'meditative thinking' is no longer of any *use* in this culture, which has reduced 'thinking' as such to a mere instrument of technological, commercial, economic and political *calculation*. In contrast to this 'calculative thinking', meditative thinking it is not a thinking focused on objects at all, nor even on the construction of objects through language. Instead of being *object-focussed* it is a thinking rooted in *field-awareness*.

"Now thinking which constructs a world of *objects* understands these objects; but meditative thinking begins with *an awareness* of the *field* within which these objects are ... *the field of awareness itself.*" [my stress]

Introduction to Heidegger's 'Discourse on Thinking' by John M. Anderson[3]

'Mentalisation'

Besides the models of psychotic structures and dynamics provided by Lacanian psychoanalysis and Kleinian 'object relations' theory (actually no less a *subject-relations* theory which in turn rests on a traditional *subject-object* relations model of consciousness) we should not forget the Marxist model. Marxist thinking of course – despite the way it long ago anticipated the 'globalisation' of capitalism – is no longer considered even *worthy* of thought because, like the meditative thinking advanced by Martin Heidegger, it has no *use-value* as object, technological tool, or source of exchange-value and profit – and because it places contemporary reality and contemporary modes of thinking in a much larger world-historical and philosophical context of no interest in a global 'United States of Amnesia'.

Instead however, we now have a new post- and neo-analytic model called 'mentalisation' – one seen as a realistic and effective approach to so-called 'borderline personality disorder', despite its psychotic dimension. 'Mentalisation' models and approaches to treatment of 'borderline personality disorders' focus on the individual's (in-)capacity to 'mentalise', in the sense of recognising and acknowledging 'other minds'. In the literature on 'mentalisation', 'mentalising' is often described as the capacity to 'be aware of', 'attend to', 'infer' or 'interpret' the subjective feelings, desires, beliefs, thoughts and intents behind both another person's outward behaviour – and one's own – and to bear both 'in mind' in relating. It is also accepted by some authors on the subject that mentalising is nothing merely 'mental' – intellectual, inferential or interpretative – but is also related to empathic, bodily feeling. Understood in this way mentalising is essentially nothing mental or intellectual at all but essentially a capacity for a form of direct *bodily* and *feeling* awareness of oneself and others.

Thus whilst it is recognised that the incapacity to adequately 'mentalise' is tantamount to *objectifying* other people, a key question raised by current, highly confused or contradictory descriptions of the mentalisation process is that 'inference' and 'interpretation' are themselves modes of objectification. Another key question raised by the mentalisation concept then, is not only *whether* but *how* an individual infers or interprets the subjective feelings and motives of others. If they do so purely in their own terms, objectifying them in service of their own motives or in a way that constitutes a mere 'projection' of their own emotions onto the other – this is not an activity of 'mentalisation' at all in the 'healthy' sense that the word is intended to imply. Any healthy mode of mentalisation must be grounded in a direct *subjective* awareness of other people's subjective or 'mental' states – and not be a mere interpretation or projection of one's own.

In the whole use of the very *term* 'mentalisation' we hear an echo of the stale old philosophical question of 'other minds'– the question of whether or how it is even possible to logical 'infer' the existence of other subjects or 'minds' behind their outward bodily form and behaviours. The problem is that the question itself rests on an old and stale but stubbornly resistant assumption – the assumption that 'mind' and 'consciousness', and with them all 'mental' or 'subjective states' are, to begin with, the function or property of isolated subjects or minds.

It is this assumption that brings with it another – the assumption that immediate experience or 'sense data' consists of a world of objects or 'objective' phenomena. 'The Awareness Principle' is a new epistemology that challenges both assumption, arguing as it does that (a) subjective awareness is *not* the private property of isolated 'subjects', and (b) that *awareness* of any and all phenomena – whether things or people – is itself something essentially *subjective*. For since all experienced phenomena are elements present or emergent within a *field* of awareness or subjectivity, they are not – even to begin with, 'objects' or 'things in themselves' – standing separate and apart from an observing 'subject', 'consciousness' or 'mind'. Thus even a physical object such as a chair in a room, is not, to begin with an 'object'. Instead it is but an element within the field of awareness – of *subjectivity* – that constitutes the very *space* of the room. It is recognition of the spacious and field character of awareness (see again Diagrams 1 and 2) that casts a wholly new light on the philosophical foundations of 'mentalisation' theory, showing it to be yet another confused and futile attempt to transcend the traditional 'subject-object' model of mind, perception and cognition *in the outmoded terms of this model* and on the basis of its still *unquestioned root assumptions*.

How then, could a new, less confused and outmoded but instead philosophically clearer and more coherent concept and model of 'mentalisation' be formulated? The first thing necessary is awareness of the *language* of current models, which equate or *conflate* 'attending to' or 'being aware' of one's own *subjective* states and those of others with *objectifying* them – thus having to 'infer' or 'interpret' their nature. The second thing is to distinguish subjectivity or awareness *as such* – what in Indian philosophy would be called 'pure awareness' – from any particular subjective phenomena or states (desires, sensations, thoughts, emotions, motives, moods etc.) that we are aware *of* or 'experience'. For the pure awareness of a thing or thought, desire or sensation, mood or motive, impulse or intent – *is not itself* a thing or thought, desire or sensation, mood or motive, impulse or intent. Awareness or subjectivity *as such* is simply the spatial field *within* which we experience or become aware of such phenomena. Only by recognising this, does it become possible not to either identify with or objectify our subjective experience of ourselves or others. This is important, because it is unaware *identification* with our own feelings – or with any element of our experience – that leads us to perceive others only from our own perspective – through the eyes and through an 'I' that is identified with our *own* feelings towards others and our experience of others – and that is therefore blind to the other's experience, their own way of feeling both themselves and others.

In this context, it is vital to recognize a fundamental distinction between 'feelings' (noun) and feeling (verb-participle). *Feelings* are something we 'have', 'experience' or are aware *of*. *Feeling* is something we *do* – as when we touch something with our hands and thereby feel both our hands and the thing that is touched. Awareness however, has an innately feeling character. To simply 'have' or 'experience' a feeling is not the same thing as being *aware* of experiencing that feeling. For it is the awareness of having a feeling, thought, desire, sensation or impulse that allows us to actively *feel* it. *Feeling* however, is not something we do with our minds but with our *bodies*. Therefore it is above all through *feeling awareness* of our own bodies, and not any 'mental' processes, that we can come to a direct bodily and feeling awareness of others and *feel* their feelings and subjective states. Only on this foundation can we begin a process of 'mentalising' or 'conceptualising' that bodily feeling awareness of self and other, doing so in a way that does not involve projecting our own feelings on to others or identifying with our own purely mental interpretations or 'inferences' *about* how they feel – both of which are often reactive defences *against* feeling our own feelings and those of others. It is such themes that take us in the direction of what I have written under the rubric of 'Awareness Based Cognitive Therapy', 'Soma-Sensitivity', 'Inner Bodywork' and 'The New Therapy' – all of which, in contrast to the whole tradition of Western philosophy and psychology, recognise *feeling* – pure feeling awareness – a *direct mode of cognition* independent of and prior to thought and mental cognition – and thus fundamental to any processes of 'mentalisation'.

In relation to 'Borderline Personality Disorder' it is recognised that one of its key symptoms is failure to recognise the emotional *effects* of one's behaviours on others. This is where the medical-psychiatric language of 'BPD' and of 'mentalisation' ignores the underlying *ethical* dimension and symptomology of abuse-rooted behaviours and their treatment. By this I mean the way in which abused individuals may display a sense of total entitlement to 'take out' their suffering on others – whether behaviourally through vocal or physical aggression and violence, by turning others into objects of their own deep-seated emotional rage, or through the most monstrous of psychical projections onto others. In all these ways they can turn the other – *any* other person – into an object of their own bad feelings or emotional outbursts, whilst as the same time perceiving the other as the 'bad subject' or cause of those feelings – and themselves as the persecutory victim *of* the other, any other. Living in a world of 'good and bad' or 'good and evil'– good and bad objects and good and bad subjects – blinds the sufferer to issues of *right or wrong* behaviours, a lesson they never learned. Having suffered abuse, they feel entitled to treat all behaviours towards them *as* abusive, and their agents as potential abusers. Their central failure of 'mentalisation' is a failure to accept the experience of benign as opposed to malign, manipulative, objectifying or abusive intent on the part of others – not just for emotional reasons but because this would undermine their unaware need and sense of ethical entitlement to abuse or attack others as they were abused and attacked. If, as a result, actual vicious circles of violent or abusive behaviour come to pass, and clinically diagnosed patients may break the law as a result, it is left to The Law to sort out the mess. Yet part of the responsibility for this unfortunate but all-too-real cycle of abuse lies with forms of treatment which fail to draw clear *ethical* boundaries or borders to 'borderline' behaviours – to 'lay down the law'. If this does not happen – or is left to late – the result may be that it is left to 'The Law' to sort out the resulting mess in way that just makes it worse – whether by arrest and punishment of patients for misdemeanours or crimes, or by their criminal abuse in the form of 'legally' and often violently enforced medication.

Without the capacity on the part of professionals to lay down strict *ethical* boundaries to the abusive 'borderline' behaviours of their patients, no amount of patience, empathy or merely psychological insight can help the sufferer to take *self-responsibility* for the reality of their own suffering – whatever its past roots or 'causes' – rather than 'taking it out' on others or projecting responsibility *for it* onto others. This 'laying down of the law' fills the gap that Lacan calls the missing 'paternal metaphor' in the world of the patient – 'the word of the father' which allows abuse-sufferers to begin to distinguish between right and wrong action – despite the failure of their own fathers, mothers or any significant others to do so. Only the establishment of clear ethical boundaries to their own 'borderline' behaviours can help abuse victim undo the consequences of their abusers' moral blindness – and prevent it becoming their own.

Referring back to Lawrence's analysis of the countless different types of 'scenario' instigated by 'borderline' individuals to maintain the symbiotic pair or dyad, he makes a particularly pertinent comment, one that implicitly highlights the dangers of purely *empathic* approaches to therapy which ignore the fundamental *ethical challenges* to the client that will *inevitably* come to the fore in the course of psychological therapies of any sort – and must be both posed by the therapist and faced by the client for therapy to succeed:

"A scenario might take any specific form and is often so subtle in appearance that it takes months for a therapist to grasp what is happening. It may take months more to find something to 'do' about it! Through *empathy and time* [my stress] the therapist becomes included in the symbiotic 'orbit' or 'membrane' of the patient by more or less *passively going along with* the patient's expressive wishes."

The whole *ethical* issue of self-responsibility and agency in illness and its relation to mentalisation-based treatment has been highlighted by a Menninger Clinic article entitled 'Agency in Illness and Recovery'[4]. The delicacy surrounding issues of agency and patient self-responsibility in relation to illness in general, and the nature of the 'compassionate criticism' that may be called for has to do in turn with the nature of agency as such. If it is seen as the activity of a pre-given agent or subject, this ignores the way in which the patient's own sense of self is not anything fixed but itself altered by somatic illness or emotional mood changes. Responsible agency on the part of a patient is not a matter of them 'pulling themselves up by their own bootstraps' but can only emerge out of *awareness* of issues of responsibility and *awareness* of the rightness or wrongness of particular actions or modes of reaction to others. For the therapeutic professional the challenge is one of cultivating this *awareness* – not simply *demanding* that the patient be 'self-responsible' agents. It is also important to respect the fact that no human being, as agent, is immune to variations in *their very sense of the self that acts* – variations that invariably accompany illness symptoms of any sort, and can become extreme.

A significant definition of 'mentalisation' as an intentional activity is that of Jeremy Holmes: "Mentalizing is seeing yourself from the outside and others from the inside." The difficulty for the paranoid individual however lies precisely in seeing themselves 'from the outside' – that is to say from the perspective of the others around them and of *their* inside. For as explained earlier, the automatic tendency is to identify the other's external view of oneself with the bad, objectifying or abusing subject. In this context, we can see the value of mentalisation-based 'treatments' based on asking questions which call upon the patient to become aware of and accept the possibility of *difference* between their *own* 'mentalisation' of the subjective states and intents behind another person's words and actions and *that of the other themselves*. Here I think of such questions as suggested by Fonagay[5:] 'Why do you think she said that?', 'What do you think he meant when he looked at you?' and 'Why do you think he behaved towards you in that way?', 'You seem to think people don't like you. Why is that?' can be helpful.

Such questions can also be seen as fundamentally distinct in principle from the more usual type of therapeutic questioning that is focused on the patient's own subjective life rather than that of significant others. Insight into the subjective life and motives, of others however, can only be *fully* experienced through the cultivation of a type of directly bodily, feeling awareness of the sensuous qualities, colourations, directions, shapes, tones and textures than make up another person's subjectivity. What might be called 'mentalising through the body' means *actively* feeling the subjective, bodily inwardness or 'soul' of another person's body with and within our own bodies – rather than (a) restricting our experience solely to our own mental or bodily 'insideness' (b) looking out at others purely from within it (c) feeling one's own body solely as a *passive* object of the other or its inwardness as subject to invasion by that of the other. Such a body-based approach to mentalisation challenges the identification of bodyhood either with the physical body as such or some form of bodily self-image. Notable in this context is that Lacan offers no concept whatsoever of the individual's inwardly felt or *subjective* body as opposed to their bodily self-image, itself supposedly derived from an externally mirrored or internalised *image* of their *physical* body. Perhaps it is for this reason that he dismissed the Eastern, non-Abrahamic 'religions', seeing them as based on an ideal and unrealisable image of 'rapport' between the sexes. Yet it precisely such a rapport that can be made *real* through neo-tantric practices which understand the roots of human gender and sexuality in the *subjectively experienced body* or 'subjective body'. It is the subjectively experienced or inwardly felt body that alone that can lead to a direct *inter-subjective experience of bodyhood* and a direct *inter-bodily experience of subjectivity.* So-called 'tantric sex' is nothing biological. It is essentially the blissful intercourse and unity of pure awareness (Shiva) and its innate vitality or 'jouissance' (Shakti). It is this unity that is signified by the hyphen in 'Shiva-Shakti' – the understanding of body, self and divinity as essentially androgynous.

The Indian tantric tradition implicitly challenges the fundamental dualism of subject and object that pervades Western metaphysics, psychology, philosophy and religion. This dualism is both rooted in and reinforces the reduction of 'awareness', 'subjectivity', 'soul' or 'psyche' to the property of an isolated 'subject', one bounded or enclosed by the 'objective' physical body and thus separate and apart from other such subjects. Such physically separate 'subjects' are by nature capable only of making mental inferences *about* the motives and emotions of others, turning them into objects of their own perceptions and emotions, or confusing the subjective states of others with their own delusory images or projections on them. It is the common delusory *imago* of ourselves and others as isolated subjects surrounded by a world of objects – and the distorted ways of relating and of 'mentalising' that go with it – that I see as the essence and core delusion behind *paranoia*. This *imago* is also the *schizoid* essence of 'borderline' states and behaviours. For behind the term 'borderline' lies the experience of a border or bodily boundary not as something that unites, bonds or 'attaches' its two sides, but as a desolate and separating war-zone, crack or fissure between them – not as something intrinsically *open and porous* – but as an iron curtain, concentration camp or ghetto of the soul.

The root assumption that subjectivity or awareness is the property of an isolated subject, one for whom its own body is but an object, perceptual image or mental self-image, is no mere *philosophical concept* but a core psychic structure, one that I believe still derives from and reinforces the basic *God-concept* of the Abrahamic religions – all of which conceive and experience the Divine as a supreme subject standing above and apart from the objects of its creation and serving as that 'ego ideal' in whose eyes all creatures feel themselves judged – and thus held in a state of paranoid anxiety. What a difference there is here from what I see as the basic tantric understanding of the Divine. In this understanding 'God' is not a being or subject 'with' awareness. Instead God *is* awareness, an unbounded subjectivity which is not the private property of any individual subject, but of which each individual's self and body is itself an individualised *portion* – thus making all they *are and experience an expression of the Divine* and not an *object* of judgement or forgiveness, mercy or punishment, use or abuse by an idealised or ideal subject, by a divinised 'ego ideal'.

Whereas in Western culture and religion, 'Law and Order' are seen as a prerogative of a patriarchal or paternal law-giver and enforcer, human or divine, in the East the fundamental cosmic and ethical 'law' determining the 'order' (Dharma) of the universe is called Karma. Yet 'Karmic Law' is not something seen as imposed or exercised by a paternal God. Nor is it essentially a mere temporal relation of cause and effect – for example wrong action leading in time to a punitive consequence. Instead it is an immediate relation of action (the root meaning of *karma*) and reaction. For just as every action has – immediately and without temporal delay – an equal and opposite reaction, so is every attack on or abuse of another an attack on or abuse of oneself. It is in this fact or 'karmic law' that lie the seeds of any temporal consequences of our acts, whether in this life or others.

Some final remarks on 'mentalisation'. Nowhere have I seen noted the way in which the mentalisation model renders paradoxical and places into question the whole practical paradigm of psychological therapies which turn the client into the centre of the universe, make the client's subjective experience the sole focus of the therapeutic dialogue or interaction – and, under the pretext of preserving the therapist's own border or 'boundaries' – effectively presents the client with a pretence that the therapist has no independent subjective life of their own not focused on that of the client or outside the framework of the therapeutic or treatment session. The paradox lies in the way that this paradigm runs counter to the central aim of encouraging the client's capacity to 'mentalise' the subjective life of significant others – for the paradigm effectively rules out the very person of the therapist *as* such a significant other. Naturally I am not suggesting that this practical paradigm should be simply reversed – placing the therapist's practical and subjective life at the centre of the therapeutic dialogue or interaction. And yet the paradox does point to what could be perceived as a central criterion for the *termination* of therapy or treatment – namely the birth and expression of an authentic, dispassionate interest in the life of the therapist on the part of the client – one not motivated by any need or desire to distract or divert attention away from the client's problems or suffering. For what else but authentic *interest* in the lives of others can provide the motivation for acknowledging and 'mentalising' their subjective life. Thus if the interest of the analyst or therapist in 'mentalising' the subjective life of the analysand or client is never, at no stage and in no way *reciprocated*, then surely this itself tells us about the *sine qua non* of the client's capacity to 'mentalise' – their *interest* in other people.

The term 'mentalisation' can and has been be taken as a synonym or neologism for many other earlier terms – 'intersubjectivity', 'object relations', 'empathy' etc. Yet what if its true foundation, like theirs, is *interest* as such, understood both in the ordinary and most essential sense of the word? For in its essence, 'interest' is a relation to others that both seeks their essence, comes from our own essence, and thus leads to a mutual and meaningful interrelation of essences: *inter-esse.* Yet whilst interest in 'objects' has long since disappeared from basic sciences such as quantum physics – the very concept of 'mass' being nothing but an abstract *mathematical* interrelationships – biological psychiatry and the whole medical-model of 'diagnosis' and 'treatment' remains the last, pseudo-scientific bastion of a profession whose practitioners are trained to apply a wholly *dis-interested* eye to the subjectively felt body and subjectively felt *dis-ease* of their patients, a disinterest still excused as a means to a spurious 'objectivity' – in reality the total reduction of the human being to the *human body* and of the latter to the physical body rather than the inwardly felt or subjective body. That is to say the human body, outer and inner, perceived from without and as an object – a mere fleshly mass of tissue – and 'treated' as such. The mentality behind medical practice and the medical model are the very opposite of 'mentalisation'. All the more important then, that attempts to subsume the latter within the former and treat it merely as a new technology of medical-model treatment – or to lend it false authority through the neuro-biological reductionism of brain science be resisted. For again, since *awareness as such* is the precondition or *field condition* for our awareness of any thing or body whatsoever, it cannot – *in principle* – be seen as the function of any thing or body that we are conscious aware *of*. Whatever old and new technologies of scanning or measurement are applied to body or brain, all they can give us is external images of brain activity displayed by instruments. They can never show us thoughts, feelings or *mental* activity *as such*. Thus though we can both directly sense and mentalise different elements of subjective experience, our own and that of others, it will remain forever impossible to reduce them to objects perceived from without by a 'subject', good or bad.

If we speak of mentalisation as a type of 'apperception' or 'apprehension' of the point of view of another it is important to remember the root meaning of these terms; apperception being precisely a pre-perceptual awareness, and apprehension a 'prehensile' awareness – an awareness that does not or has not yet 'grasped' (*prae-hendere*) something as if it were an object. Such an 'apperceptive' *awareness*, both of ourselves and our own subjective states and those of others, cannot – *in principle* – be the *property* of any self or other we are *aware of*. The sole exception is that self, identified in the tantric tradition, which does not 'possess' but *is* awareness (Chaitanyatman).

If Bion's mantra was 'thoughts without a thinker', then the mantra of 'The Awareness Principle', understood as a neo-tantric metaphysics and psychology, is 'subjectivity without a subject'. The Awareness Principle defines the 'unconscious' precisely *as* an unbounded, 'subject-less' *field* of subjectivity or awareness (Shiva) albeit one which is the common foundation and source of all individualised 'consciousness' (Jivas). The doctrinal association of tantra with triadic constructs (Trika) and its cultural association with 'transgressive sacrality'[6] and sexuality gives it special significance in relation to Lacan's re-interpretation of the Oedipal triad as a fundamental structure of the psyche and not simply a development phase of childhood determined by the incest taboo or its transgression. Then again, it is important to understand that Tantrism cannot simply be opposed to Western religions and subsumed within the traditional Eastern 'Dharmic' faiths such as Hinduism, Buddhism and Jainism, but constitutes a distinctive tradition in its own right that found expression in them all – a tradition that corresponds and contributed to the heterodox 'Gnostic' traditions of Judaeo-Christianity and Islam.

If Lacan's mantra, signified in religious terms, is 'The Word become Flesh' – literally 'the speech of the other' inscribed in the patient's body as their symptoms (in the same way that Tantric practice is seen as inscribing initiatory Mantra in the body of the neophyte) then his later substitution of the word 'symptom' with its historic antecedent – 'sinthome' – becomes even more pertinent in this connection. Lacan had long understood the symptom as "inscribed in a writing process", but his reading of James Joyce led him to see how Joyce found through his writing a way of organising his private *jouissance* – expressing intense, quasi-mystical epiphanies in a way that both defied any need for analysis.

> "The move from conceiving of the symptom as a message which can be deciphered by reference to the unconscious 'structured like a language' to seeing it as the trace of the particular modality of the subject's *jouissance*, culminates in the introduction of the term *sinthome*. Far from calling for some analytic dissolution the *sinthome* is what allows one to live by providing a unique organization of *jouissance*. The aim of the cure is to identify with the *sinthome*."

"Thus Joyce becomes a *saint homme* who by refusing any imaginary solution, was able to invent a procedure of using language to organize *jouissance*."[7]

Dylan Evans, *Dictionary of Lacanian Psychoanalysis*

Through the *sinthome,* Lacan admits of a uniquely individual quality of *jouissance* which he represents topologically, by a fourth 'ring' knotting the three realms of the Real, Imaginary and Symbolic, and as such transcending analysis or 'subjection' to 'the Symbolic'.

"The theoretical shift from linguistics to topology which marks the final period of Lacan's work constitutes the true status of the *sinthome* as unanalysable … The 1975-6 seminar extends the theory of the Borromean Knot, which in the previous seminar had been proposed as the structure of the subject, by adding the *sinthome* as the fourth ring to the triad of the real, symbolic and imaginary…" (ibid)

This fourth ring corresponds to what in traditional tantra itself is called 'Turya' – a transcendental 'fourth' beyond the three realms of waking, sleeping and dreaming awareness – yet without the dimension of irreducible individuality that Lacan attached to the *sinthome.* I understand *this* dimension as a unique grouping of innate *sensual tones, textures and qualities of subjective awareness*, comparable to what Heidegger called 'fundamental moods', yet unique to the individual – pervading, like moods, both their lived experience ('the Real'), their language ('the Symbolic') and their creative Imagination and at the same time capable of linking the individual through 'mystical' feeling, imagery and symbols with particular qualities of the universal or divine awareness – for example the experience of awareness as 'light'. Lacan's 'sinthome' is in this sense a new and central signifier cognate with the root meaning of 'tantra' as 'loom' in tantric terms themselves the Great Loom of Life which is the true 'unconscious' – a universal 'super-conscious' subjectivity (albeit one without a pre-given subject) which finds ever-changing expression in individual subjectivity or 'consciousness'. Understood as a unique *individual* 'weave' of *particular* sensual tones, textures, colourations and shapes of the divine or *universal* awareness – lived through with the inwardly felt or subjective body – the *sinthome* is the loom or 'tantra' of both directly felt sense and verbal signification, lived experience and language. By the same token, to understand 'cure' of symptoms as *identification* with the 'sinthome' and its unique individual *jouissance* takes us beyond the realm of psychoanalytic and neo-analytic treatments to that of traditional tantra and the neo-tantric world view I articulated through 'The New Yoga' – the Principle and Practice of awareness. For in Tantric terms, identifying with the *sinthome* means identifying with the individual qualities of subjective awareness or *jouissance* behind all symptoms – qualities which are at the same time individualised expressions and embodiments (Shaktis) of a or divine *awareness* (Shiva).

If, as Buddhism claims, 'life is suffering', then to end suffering would be to end or extinguish *life* through 'Nirvana' – which means to extinguish or 'blow out'. The alternative is to choose, with awareness, to *be* one's suffering, not through enacting it in the form of pathological behaviours but by identifying with the aliveness of feeling awareness that the suffering is there to *keep* alive. *Being* our suffering we no longer experience it merely *as* a passive suffering of pathological symptoms (passivity being the root meaning of suffering as *pathos*). Being our suffering we allow the symptoms we otherwise passively suffer to transform into the *sinthome* – into felt qualities of subjective vitality or *jouissance* that no longer require *symptoms as their signifiers. This* 'transformation' is the central link between the precepts and practice of Lacanian analysis and 'The Awareness Principle' – the neo-tantric precepts and practices that together constitute what I call 'The New Yoga of Awareness'.

218

References:

1   *The Shadow of the Object: Psychoanalysis of the Unthought Known*
    Bollas, C Free Association Books 1987
2   *Listening Perspectives in Psychotherapy* Hedges, Lawrence Jason
    Aronson 1991
3   *A Theory of Thinking* in *Second Thoughts: Selected Papers on
    Psychoanalysis* Bion, W Karnac Books, 1984
4   *Discourse on Thinking*, Martin Heidegger, Harper and Row, 1966
5   *Agency in Illness and Recovery*, Allen, J.G., Munich, R.L. and
    Rogan, A. (2004). The Menninger Clinic and the Menninger
    Department of Psychiatry and Behavioral Sciences, Baylor
    College of Medicine
6   *Psychotherapy for Borderline Personality Disorder, Mentalization-Based
    Treatment* Bateman A, Fonagy P (2004) Oxford University Press,
    Oxford.
7   *Transgressive Sacrality in Hinduism and the World Religions*
    Sunthar Visuvalinga www.svabhinava.org/tshwr/default.html
8   *Dictionary of Lacanian Psychoanalysis*, Dylan Evans Routledge 1996

Bibliography:

Melanie Klein *Envy and Gratitude*
                Love, Hate and Reparation
Jacques Lacan *Ecrits* translated by Bruce Fink
                The Four Fundamental Concepts of Psychoanalysis
                translated by Alan Sheridan

Focal, Local and Field Awareness

Diagram 1: 'Focal Awareness'. Contents of consciousness, focussed on and objectified by an 'ego' or 'I' which experiences neither itself nor its objects as expressions of a field of awareness, but sees those objects as separate and apart from one another - and experiences itself as a localised subject of consciousness separate and apart from its objects. (p. 122)

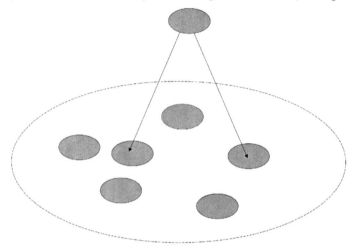

Diagram 2: 'Local Awareness'. Contents of an awareness field experienced solely from the perspective of a centre or 'locus' of awareness constituted by *one* dominant element within that field with which we are identified (for example, experiencing a feeling solely 'through the lens' of one particular thought or from the perspective of one particular experienced aspect of ourselves).

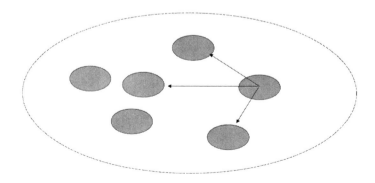

Diagram 3: 'Field Awareness' – elements of our experience (sensations or emotions, thoughts or things) experienced within and as a part of a spacious, non-localised *field* of awareness.

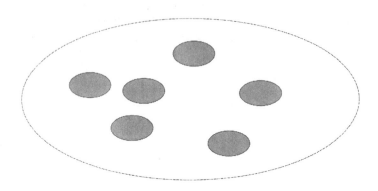

Diagram 3: 'Field Attention' – attending to a localised element of our experience *from within* and *as a part* of a larger field of awareness. Attending from Field Awareness rather than from Local Awareness.

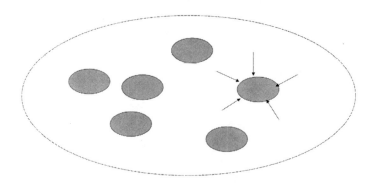

Diagram 5: Field Awareness as both *transcendent and immanent* – the awareness field (white) experiencing itself as not only embracing and transcending but also as immanent within and pervading all of its localised elements (white areas within the ovoids). This enables each element of our experience – anything we are aware of – to be experienced *as* an awareness in its own right. A thought, feeling or sensation for example, is not just something there is an awareness *of* – it *is* an awareness of something in its own right.

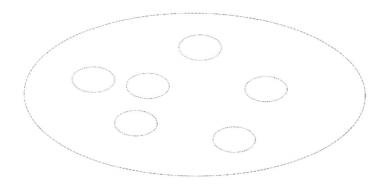

Diagram 6: Field Awareness as an awareness embracing both actually present elements of experience (grey ovoids) and potential or emergent elements of experience (hatched ovoids).

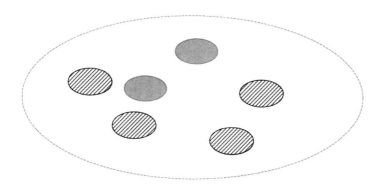

Field Awareness and the Nature of 'Projective Identification'

If we do not conceive of individual 'mind' or consciousness as the property of a punctiform subject located somewhere in his or her head or brain, but instead as a field of awareness, and conceive the essence bodyhood, not as a physical object bounding an individual's awareness, but as a boundary-field or field-boundary *of* awareness – then we can also generate a newer and truer model of 'projective identification'. This is a model that does not assume or imply the existence of separate subjects, psyches or consciousnesses – one of whom projects or expels 'internal' objects from within itself whilst the other 'internalises' or has them projected 'into' them. This crude model is pictured below

Diagram 3

Self   **Other**

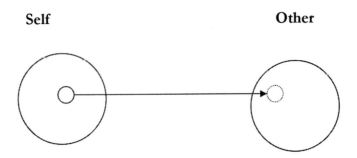

An alternative model of intersubjectivity and projective identification (Diagram 4) is based on the idea not of separated subjects but of overlapping *fields of awareness* – thus creating an area of overlap which is the *intersubjective field*. For here, as in Diagram 2 (see Introduction) the larger circles representing each individual are

224

to be understood as *fields* of pure awareness or subjectivity, each of which embraces all elements or 'contents' of their subjective experience (the smaller circles). These elements of experience include not only perceptions, thoughts and emotions but also each individual's experience of their own body and other bodies. The larger circle represent not only each individual's awareness field as a whole but their larger body – essentially nothing but a non-physical 'field boundary' or 'field body' of awareness – their 'awareness body'.

Diagram 4

Self   **Other**

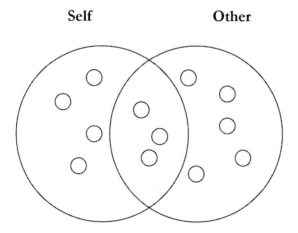

Using this model as foundation, the process of 'projective identification' does not require the movement or 'projection' of an 'internal object' (in reality but an element of subjective experience) from one individual to another. Instead the 'projective' process is itself nothing but an *identification* of the intersubjective field of overlap of Self and Other, and of any shared element of subjective experience within that field – whether felt as a good or bad 'object'

– solely *with* the other and *not* with the self – as in Diagram 5. Here, a *shared element* of subjective experience (the small hatched circle) is not so much 'projected' as identified solely with the other, seen as contained within *their* psyche, subjectivity or awareness field alone, rather than felt as an element within the field of overlap or *intersubjective field*. 'Projective identification' then, is thus both an act of *dis-identification* from any element of experience *shared* by Self and Other within the intersubjective field – and its *identification* solely *with* the Other.

Diagram 5

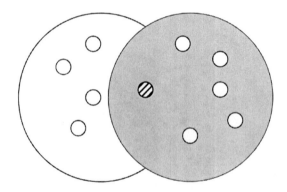

Notice how the result is a contraction of the 'projecting' individual's own field of awareness – a loss not only of any element of their experience treated as a 'bad object' but also of any 'good' elements of their subjective experience previously shared within the *intersubjective field*. This is a new way of illustrating how the process of 'projective identification' can result in a sense of losing parts of oneself, or indeed whole 'areas' of subjective awareness. Diagram 5 also illustrates the converse process of internalizing or 'introjecting' an element of another's subjective experience. For the individual whose awareness field is represented by the grey circle may also *occlude* the intersubjective field of overlap between Self and Other, thus treating one or more elements within this field purely as part of their own field – belonging solely to their own psyche and subjective identity.

What none of these purely dyadic diagrams fully bring into prominence however, is the *trans-personal* space or field of pure or transcendental awareness *around* the two circles, one that embraces *both* Self and Other within it. This surrounding space is a singular, all-embracing and universal field of 'pure' trans-personal or 'transcendental' awareness of the sort recognised in Indian thought as the very essence of the Divine – and of which all things and all persons are an individualised portion and expression.

Part 6

Awareness and Somatic Illness

Subjectively, illness of any sort does not begin with some external or internal cause – some object such as a virus or cancerous cell. Nor does it even necessarily begin with some well-defined experiential symptom such as a localised pain. Instead it begins with an ill-defined *awareness* of 'not feeling ourselves'. It is this awareness of 'not feeling ourselves' that is accompanied by worries and experienced as a sense of 'dis-ease'. And whilst it is common knowledge that illness can 'change' people, what medicine ignores is that the very essence of illness has to do with *identity* – every symptom being subjectively experienced both as an altered *state of consciousness* and as an altered *sense of self*. If ignored, the ill-defined awareness of 'not feeling ourselves' can grow and take the form of a more localised well-defined symptom. 'Scientific' medicine then seeks objective causes and cures for such symptoms. Yet it implicitly retains a subjective element. This is not just because it relies partly on patients' subjective accounts of their symptoms but also because 'cure' – indeed 'health' as such – is understood not just as an absence, or successful elimination or amelioration of symptoms but also as a restored sense of *identity* – 'feeling ourselves' again.

The entire medical understanding of illness and the entire relationship of patient and physician rests on an unspoken agreement to seek something *other than self* (whether an organic cause, traumatic event, or a diagnostically labelled 'disorder') to explain the patient's sense of dis-ease, their awareness of *not feeling themselves*. The basic principle of medicine – 'The Medical Principle' – is based not on *fact* but on (a) the dogmatic *belief* that illness has no intrinsic meaning for the individual and (b) the military *metaphor* of 'fighting' its causes rather than seeking its meaning. In contrast The Awareness Principle offers an approach to illness which begins where it actually begins – the sense of 'dis-ease' which accompanies the awareness of 'not feeling ourselves'. Yet instead of denying meaning to this inwardly felt dis-ease – merely labelling it as a medical disease or disorder and seeking causes for it in something *other than self* – The Practice of Awareness encourages the patient to fully affirm the awareness of *not feeling themselves* as soon as it emerges, and to both *understand* and *transform* it into a quite different awareness – the awareness of *feeling another self.* This can both prevent the ill-defined dis-ease of not feeling oneself from developing into well-defined disease symptoms, or alternatively allow those very symptoms to be experienced in a different way – not simply as an altered mental or physical state but as an altered state of consciousness and with it an altered bodily *sense of self.*

By fully affirming this altered sense of self, we let the essential dis-ease of *not feeling ourselves* achieve its true and most meaningful purpose – that of allowing us to *feel another self* – one we hitherto feared to be aware of or to recognise as part of our *self as a whole* – our 'soul'. And by letting another self express itself in our thoughts and emotions and finding ways to *body* it in our overall demeanour or 'body language', we remove the need to *repress* or medicalise our bodily sense of that self. For then that self will no longer feel forced to *express* itself through bodily symptoms or through behaviours regarded as forms of 'mental' disorder.

We do not 'have' a body. We body 'our-selves'. Our bodies are but the embodiment of the particular way in which we are bodying ourselves – and the particular selves we are bodying. Being aware of an emotion or any aspect of our self-experience and *bodying* it in our demeanour is not the same as 'somatising' it through physical symptoms or giving it free reign to emotionally determine our *behaviour.* Someone who cannot allow themselves to *frown* with anger, adopt an aggressive bearing or give an angry or aggressive *look* to someone – thus silently *embodying* that anger through their demeanour – is more likely to *enact* their anger in their behaviour, expressing it in harsh or hurtful words or deeds. Thus someone who cannot allow themselves to be fully *aware* of their anger and feel it in their bodies – to *be* angry – is more likely to 'get' angry. It is only because we are not taught, like good actors, to first of all *inwardly* feel the selves that find expression in the different 'parts' they act out – without in anyway *judging* them – that we ourselves may feel forced to act those parts in real life, or feel a strong *fear* of doing so. The reason that the actor Anthony Hopkins could so effectively play the gruesome figure of Hannibal Lecter – without becoming or acting like him in real life – is *not* because he distanced himself as a person from the part he played but because he deliberately sought, found and felt the self within him that could fully identify with Hannibal.

People fear to fully feel any 'other selves' that they judge as 'bad' or 'dangerous' in some way – for example mad, violent, sadistic, weak or suicidal selves. The fear is that if they allowed themselves to be more aware of these selves and feel them more fully, they would *become* mad, violent, sadistic, weak, suicidal etc. In reality it is those who fear to feel such selves within themselves who are more likely to end up impulsively 'acting out' these selves in their behaviour. Thus a self that feels violent only actually acts in a violent way through the body if its violence is not fully felt in a bodily way. Actual bodily violence results from a *fear* of violent feelings, and is essentially a last-ditch attempt to *evacuate* violent feelings *from* one's body rather than fully feeling them with and within one's body. Bodily *enactment* of feared emotions, impulses, states and selves replaces a fuller awareness of those emotions, impulses, states and selves. That is a great paradox, for were we to allow ourselves greater awareness, that very awareness would *free* us from those aspects of our bodily self-experience that we fear.

For paradoxically, *awareness* of our bodies is not itself anything bodily but is a bodiless or body-free awareness. Similarly the awareness of our minds is not itself anything 'mental' but is a mind-free awareness. The same basic precept of The Awareness Principle applies to all aspects of our self-experience – including our thoughts, feelings, fears, sensations, impulses, illnesses and sickness symptoms. Just as *the awareness* of a thought is not itself a thought, and is something essentially thought-free, so also is the awareness of an emotion, sensation, urge or impulse something essentially free of emotions, sensations, urges or impulses. There is nothing sick or ill about the *awareness* of a symptom or the awareness of feeling ill. Similarly, the awareness of a fear is not itself something fearful but is essentially a 'neutral' or fear-free awareness. And just as the awareness of our bodies is nothing bodily, so is the awareness of a particular self not something that binds us to that self – or to any self.

It is only because we do not allow ourselves to be more aware of other selves and the bodily states that express them that we can *neither* free ourselves from them – recognising that the very awareness of them is distinct and free from them – *nor* fully affirm and body these selves as valid ways of feeling ourselves. The suffering associated with illness arises because, instead of affirming the selves we feel when we are ill, however 'foreign' they may feel to our usual sense of self, we feel 'possessed' or plagued by them – whether in the form of somatic illness or uncontrolled emotions, thoughts, inner voices or behaviours. At the same time we see the cause of such symptoms as something essentially *other than self* – whether another person, a 'malign spirit' or a 'foreign body' such as a virus, toxin or cancerous cell. Not feeling ourselves, we blame our illness on this 'other'. In this way we deprive ourselves of the opportunity to become aware of another self within us, and to both face and overcome our fears of it through that very awareness.

The Awareness Principle allows us to affirm our most elementary experience of illness as an awareness – an *awareness* of feeling our own bodies or minds as having become something 'foreign' to us, no longer fitting our previous sense of identity or self. The Medical Principle blames illness on 'foreign bodies'. Yet this is just the same as blaming the ills of society on *foreigners* – rather than seeing them as a new and healthy element of the social body, whose values can help make it more balanced and 'whole'. If we seek the causes of illness in 'foreign bodies', and seek to chemically or surgically root them out or 'eliminate' them we are acting like xenophobes or little Hitlers. Worse still, we are actively *encouraging* that which feels foreign to us – either within our own soul or within society – to take the malignant form of either illness or social ills. The Nazi state was a Medical State – one in which The Medical Principle was applied to all social problems, all of which were seen by Hitler as 'diseases' of the social 'body' or 'Volk', and blamed on racially foreign, impure or genetically unfit bodies – in particular Jews, Gypsies and the mentally or physically 'handicapped'. The 'Final Solution' to social ills was seen as a medical one – the clinical *annihilation* of all people and ideas seen as detrimental to the health of the social body. Yet like German rocket scientists, German Nazi physicians, eugenicists, psychiatrists and pharmaceutical companies played a key role in the development of *today's* 'genetic' medicine and pharmaceutical drug therapies. Nazi social 'health fascism' is reflected today in the growth of state-imposed health regulations and treatment 'regimes'. Those who seek alternative forms of healing in 'complementary' medicine on the other hand, do not realise that these are as much based on The Medical Principle and a 'Medical Model' of illness as orthodox medicine. Which is why not only vegetarianism or vehement anti-smoking campaigns, but also the promotion of exercise, herbal and homoeopathic remedies were as much a part of Nazi ideology as they are a part of today's health fads and 'health fascism'. The only *truly* alternative medicine is one whose basic principle – The Awareness Principle – challenges The Medical Principle and 'The Medical Model' of illness as such.

ILLNESS INSTEAD OF AWARENESS	AWARENESS INSTEAD OF ILLNESS
A personal secretary finds herself stuck in a job with a bullying and abusive boss. Fearing to express her feelings of irritation, anger and embarrassed humiliation 'face to face' and 'face up to' her boss, feeling vulnerable in the face of the unpredictable rage this might unleash in her boss, and afraid with good reason that it might be 'rash' to risk her job by doing so, she keeps 'a straight face' in the face of all the bullying. Over time her feelings come to the surface in her body itself – in the form of an 'irritating' and 'angry' red skin rash. Lacking a way to face her boss, let alone 'whack him one' – even though she is itching to do so – the rash appears on her face, arms and hands. Plagued by itching, she scratches and irritates her own skin until it blisters and bleeds – an activity that provides, unaware to herself, some satisfaction in releasing her 'bad blood' towards her boss. But her feelings of embarrassment and shame about not being able to face up to her boss become displaced by shame and embarrassment about the rash itself. So she goes to her doctor.	A personal secretary, faced with having to work with a bullying and abusive boss for the first time in her career, doesn't 'feel herself' at work in the way she was used to doing. She allows herself to be fully aware of her emotions of anger, vulnerability, shame and humiliation – and yet is wary of rashly letting them out in an emotional outburst that might risk her job. On a day-to-day basis she reminds herself that the awareness of an emotion, however intense is not itself an emotion or impulse but something emotion- and impulse-free. This makes her feel less vulnerable to her boss's bullying and less impelled to react emotionally to it in a rash way. Instead she sees the bullying abusiveness for what it is – as the indirect expression of a deep insecure and vulnerable self in her boss. Nevertheless, she stays with her awareness of her own emotions, allowing herself to fully affirm and feel them in her body. As a result they condense into a bodily sense of a completely different self within her, a self that feels inwardly strong enough to face up to her boss – or to anyone –

Not even thinking that asking her questions about her *life world* might have any diagnostic significance, the doctor is therefore completely blind to the metaphorical *meaning* of her 'angry rash'. Applying The Medical Principle, the doctor's sole interest is in diagnosing the rash as some form of skin disorder, the 'cause' of which must for him be some impersonal 'thing' – even though there is in this case no 'thing' to explain it such as a liver disorder. Nevertheless he prescribes a cortisone cream to 'treat' and 'cure' her problem. The problem is that she then becomes dependent on the cream, which far from helping her to become tougher and more 'thick-skinned' emotionally, has the side-effect of thinning her actual skin surface itself, making it more vulnerable to embarrassing sores and bleeding. Eventually she feels forced to take more sick leave and then to leave the job altogether and seek another boss.

and challenge them in a calm, non-reactive but nevertheless firm and resolute way. By simply letting herself feel this other self in a bodily way and give it expression through her body language and tone of voice she feels ever less vulnerable, and instead becomes even more aware of the vulnerability that lies behind her boss's bullying. Sensing this new self and awareness in her, her boss finds it strangely more difficult to be as bullying towards her as before. Now it is her boss who is uncomfortably aware of feeling another self, a less powerful and more vulnerable self. Afraid of this self, her boss reacts by actively intensifying the abusive bullying, only to find it met by a calm, resolute and firmly toned response from the secretary. Yet her boss now feels so secretly ashamed of bullying the secretary that she is not fired. She does not develop a rash, feels ready to face up to bullying, and as a result does not feel vulnerable, shamed or humiliated.

Healing through Awareness 1

1. If you are feeling unwell do not think to yourself that 'you' are feeling unwell, or that 'you' are experiencing this or that physical-mental state or symptom.

2. Do not even ask *why* you are feeling the way you are, but *who – which you* – is feeling that way.

3. Be aware not just of what or how 'you' are feeling but how and who it makes *you* feel – the sense of self that it induces.

4. Be aware of your state of being not simply as a mental or physical state but as a distinct self or 'self-state' – a distinct *you*.

5. Remind yourself also that your current mental and physical state is but one of many 'self-states' among others, one self or *you* among many others.

6. Now identify with that self which is distinct from each and every *you* – for it is nothing but the very *awareness* of any and every self-state that can be experienced.

7. Feel this self – the *awareness self* – as a spacious field or pure centre of awareness that is absolutely *distinct* both from your current self-state or *you* and from all such self-states.

8. Choose to allow *the you* that your current state of being is bringing to the fore to *express* itself *more* fully – both in your bodily language and in your thoughts and emotions.

9. Do not try to heal or change the self or *you* that is expressing itself through your current state or symptoms but let it gradually *change* you – allowing it to alter the way you feel your self as a whole – your whole self or 'soul'.

10. Do not become 'a patient' but *be patient*. For by letting your mental-physical states and symptoms *change you* – which means feeling and expressing the *other selves* that they express – those selves will gradually no longer need to express *themselves* through states or symptoms of 'illness'.

Illness as an Awareness

Every feeling, symptom, mental or physical state, together with our overall sense of self or 'self-state' is not just something we are aware *of*. Its meaning lies in the fact that *it is itself an awareness* of something. Thus a head or neck ache, though we aware *of* it as a bodily tension itself *embodies an awareness* of something beyond it – for example an awareness of real personal tensions in our lives, relationships or place of work.

Just as a person whose family has been made homeless or wiped out in a war has *good reasons* for feeling 'depressed', so do all feelings – including feeling 'depressed', 'anxious', 'angry' or 'ill' – have good reasons. They are not just programmed or mechanical physiological reactions to or 'effects' of external or internal 'causes'. Simply to label feelings as 'positive' or 'negative', to describe ourselves as 'well' or 'unwell', or to call the way we feel as 'good' or 'bad', is to deny the inherent *meaning* of all feelings – as an awareness of something beyond themselves. Symptoms of illness, like dream symbols, are a form of *condensed* awareness. Their *inherently* positive value and meaning lies in helping us to become more *directly* aware of what it is that they themselves *are* a condensed or embodied awareness of. Thus digestive problems are a condensed embodied awareness of an aspect of our lives or lived experience of the world we find difficult to 'stomach' or 'digest'.

Even though illness is often or mainly experienced through *localised* bodily symptoms (including 'mental' states such as a sense of confusion localised in our heads), every such symptom is also and always accompanied by a state of consciousness or 'mood' that pervades *our entire body* and in this way also affects our entire *bodily sense of self*. This bodily sense of self or 'self-state' is itself an undifferentiated *awareness* of what may be many different aspects of our overall *life world* that are difficult or uncomfortable, distressing or disturbing for us – thus giving rise to a general sense of 'dis-ease'. That is why, in order to find meaning in the overall bodily sense of 'unwellness' or 'dis-ease' that accompanies a specific illness, it is necessary first to experience it *as* a *self-state* – to be aware of how it imparts an overall colour, mood and texture to our bodily sense of self, one which in turn colours our experience of our whole *life world*. To pass from an experience of illness as 'not feeling ourselves' to one of 'feeling another self' – a distinct self or 'self-state' – means experiencing this distinct bodily sense of self. The 'other self' we experience through illness however is, by definition, *an experienced self* – a self we are aware *of*. Our self as a whole or 'soul' on the other hand, is not essentially any *experienced* self, symptom, state of consciousness or 'self-state', but rather the very *awareness* of experiencing it. To avoid becoming unconsciously identified with the self-states and symptoms of dis-ease, it is necessary to identify with that 'whole self' which is nothing *but* this awareness – the *experiencing self* rather than any *experienced self*. Only within the awareness that *is* this self – our 'awareness self' – can we in turn feel and affirm every particular feeling and self we experience or are aware *of*. We are as much aware of our *self as a whole* – our soul – as we are aware of our *body* as a whole. Yet the 'body' of our whole self or soul – our *awareness self* – is not just our physical body but *our entire life world*. For, it is an awareness that embraces everything and 'everybody' in our world, from our immediate present reality and relationships to our past and future – and ultimately the entire universe.

The *second* step in healing ourselves through awareness is therefore to experience each and every localised bodily sensation or symptom, no matter how subtle, *as* an *awareness* of some specific aspect of our larger body – of our life world. Thus by giving more awareness to a localised muscular tension we can experience it *as* an awareness of a specific tension in our life world. Through a meditational process of giving awareness to each and every *localised* bodily feeling or sensation of dis-ease – no matter how subtle, and by making sure we attend to each and every *region* of our body in the process – we can come to experience each of these feelings and sensations *as* an awareness of some aspect of our larger body or life world. Through this process we are literally putting ourselves together – 're-membering' and making whole that larger body that is our life world *as a whole*. And by simply *granting* awareness to each region of our bodies and each sensation or feeling of dis-ease or discomfort we experience within it, our overall sense of dis-ease and overall 'self-state' will automatically begin to alter. For we will feel ever-more pervaded, lightened and healed by that very self which is the *awareness* we grant – both to our overall self-state *and* to the specific, localised feelings and sensations it unites – that 'whole self' which *is* nothing but the pure, healing light of *awareness as such*, one which pervades the entire universe and every body in it.

Healing through Awareness 2

1. Give yourself time to attend to your immediate bodily sense of any discomfort, tension or emotional feeling – however intense or delicate and subtle – that you are aware of. Be more aware of where and how you feel it in your body.

2. Staying aware of any such localised sensation or feeling of dis-ease, remind yourself that it is itself an awareness of some aspect of your life-world and relationships that is a source of unease or 'dis-ease'.

3. Wait until a spontaneous awareness arises of what specific aspect of your life-world it is that the sensation or feeling of dis-ease embodies.

4. Grant awareness to one localised sensation or feeling of dis-ease or discomfort after another, staying with it long enough until it too recalls you to some specific aspect of your life world, present, past or future.

5. Take time to follow this process through - making sure you attend to every region of your body *in* the process – until your *overall* sense of dis-ease lifts and your overall sense of your self and body alters - feeling lightened and pervaded by the very awareness you are granting it.

The Body as a Language of Awareness

When we speak of someone 'losing heart', feeling 'disheartened' or 'heart-broken' we are not just using the language of a biological 'organ' – in this case the heart – as a metaphor for a psychological state of 'dis-ease'. It is the other way round. Heart disease is itself *a living biological metaphor* of psychic states of dis-ease such as feeling 'heart-broken', 'heartless' or 'cold-hearted'. Similarly, respiratory disorders such as asthma arise from feeling 'stifled' or 'having no room to breathe', and digestive disorders from aspects of our lives we do not feel able to 'stomach' or 'digest' in our awareness. The 'body language' used in phrases such as 'hard to stomach' in other words, are not 'mere' mental metaphors. Instead they point in a quite literal way to incapacities or states of dis-ease belonging to our subjectively felt body or *psychical body* – and how these in turn can find metaphorical expression in organic diseases and dysfunctions of our *physical body*.

The Medical Principle seeks 'organic' causes for illness in dysfunctions of our *biological organs*, and sees even psychical states and disorders as the result of such organic dysfunctions. As a result, medicine is blind to the deeper meaning and truth of the bodily 'metaphors' we use to describe psychical feelings and states – which are a way of recognising that the physical body and its biological organs are themselves a *living metaphorical language* of the soul or psyche – of awareness. In contrast to The Medical Principle, The Awareness Principle recognises all physical body organs and their functions as biological embodiments of our psychic body and psychical capacities. The human psychical body or 'soul body' is our awareness body – that body with which we breathe, stomach, digest, absorb and let circulate and give physical expression to our *awareness* of all we experience.

Biological organs such as lungs, stomach and heart and their corresponding *physiological functions* are localised biological expressions of these *psychical capacities*, which are essentially *capacities of awareness*. It is the absence or dysfunctioning of these *capacities* of awareness – for example our capacity to breathe, digest, metabolise, absorb, let circulate and give expression to awareness in muscular activity – that finds metaphorical expression in 'organic', biological dysfunctions, not the other way round. It is these psychic capacities of awareness that find living biological expression in our physical body organs and organic 'functions' such as respiration, digestion and circulation, just as it is psychic incapacities that find expression in organic, biological dysfunctions or disorders. In other words, it is not illness that *incapacitates* us. Instead it is failure to fully or properly exercise our *psychical capacities* – awareness – that results in incapacitating illness.

Our *biology* has its basis in our *biography*, and in that larger *body of awareness* that is our *life world* as a whole. For it is always within the specific contexts of our life world that we experience 'dis-ease', just as it is *capacities of awareness* that allow us to relate to and respond to our life world in a healthy way – *with* awareness.

Illness can and has been understood in many ways: in a purely objective and biomedical way, as a mechanical neuro-physiological 'effect' of psychical stress or trauma, as a relation to our life world and other people in it, as a form of silent bodily *communication* or even protest, as blocked action or communication, and/or as a metaphorical *language* through which we give silent bodily *expression* to any *subjectively* felt 'dis-ease'. Understanding illness as a metaphorical *language of awareness* embraces all other understandings of it. More importantly it provides us with an understanding of illness that affirms its innate *meaningfulness* in the life of the individual – as an expression and embodiment of their lived experience of themselves and of their life world as a whole, as an expression and embodiment of the degree of awareness they bring to their experience, and as an expression and embodiment too, of the specific capacities or 'organs' of awareness that they do or do not exercise in relating and responding to their experienced self and world – for it is these specific capacities that offer new keys to diagnosing illness *as* a 'language of awareness'.

Appendices

Meditation or Medication?

A Health Warning

Warning! Your clients' symptoms may well be 'iatrogogenic' – side-effects or withdrawal symptoms resulting in common, legally prescribed medications that are or were used to 'treat' them.

Recent decades have seen an enormous rise in the number of people treated with psychopharmaceutical medications – all of which have a direct effect on brain functioning. Such medications include:

Antidepressants – now prescribed for a whole range of newly classified 'disorders'.

Anxiolytics – for treating anxiety, sleep problems and panic attacks.

Neuroleptics – for treating so-called 'psychotic' symptoms.

Stimulants – used on an increasing scale to treat children with 'difficult' behaviour or so-called 'Attention Deficit Disorder'.

What is not so well known is that many of the psychological and somatic symptoms treated by counsellors and psychotherapists, physicians and psychiatrists are a direct result of taking or having taken medications of these sorts. Symptoms such as depression, anxiety, sleep disturbances panic attacks, phobias, compulsions, mania, poor concentration, loss of affect, suicidal thoughts and psychotic episodes are all recognised by pharmaceutical themselves companies themselves as potential effects of the very medications designed to treat them.

According to the psychiatrist Peter Breggin, health practitioners now confront a hidden epidemic of iatrogenic (medically caused) psychical and somatic illness resulting from short or long-term chemical disruption of brain functioning. The adverse effects of psychopharmaceutical medications, both acute and chronic, include:

- intended effects (for example the mind-numbing depression of brain functioning and the dulling of thought and emotion induced by *neuroleptics*).

- paradoxical effects (the accentuation of the very symptoms which the drugs were prescribed to treat, such as panic attacks induced by *anxiolytics*).

- physiological side effects (ranging from respiratory, cardiac, gastrointestinal problems to long-term brain and liver damage, peripheral nerve damage, sexual dysfunction, weight gain, chronic fatigue or dyskinesia (uncontrolled Parkinsonian-type movements).

- psychological side effects (symptoms of mania, depression, panic attacks, psychotic episodes, suicidal ideation etc. of a sort not previously experienced by the individual at any time before taking the medications).

- withdrawal effects (acute or chronic psychological and physiological effects experienced when coming off prescribed medications).

- tolerance effects (needing ever-increasing dosages of the same drug to simply avoid acute and frightening withdrawal effects).

- short and long-term dependency (addiction as a result of tolerance and withdrawal effects).

There is a tendency to interpret even the most dangerous physiological side-effects – if reported – merely as symptoms of a patient's psychological disorder. Cardiac symptoms, for example, may be interpreted as 'anxiety' symptoms, rather than the other way round. As a result, patients with genuine cardiac problems may remain medically untested and untreated until they suffer a serious heart attack.

Many social workers, nurses, counsellors, psychotherapists and alternative health practitioners however, still believe that the use and efficacy of psychopharmaceutical drugs is scientifically proven.

The medical myth has it that mental disorders such as 'depression' are caused by biochemical imbalances in the brain.. Not only has there never been any scientific evidence of this whatsoever, it is actually not technically possible to measure the levels of neurotransmitters in the synapses between brain cells. The hypothesis of an original 'chemical imbalance' was arrived at by arguing backwards from the supposedly therapeutic effects of drugs designed to chemically influence the release or reuptake of particular neurotransmitters – thereby altering their respective levels in the brain, even though the latter cannot be directly measured. Thus whilst there is no evidence that such drugs correct imbalances in the brain, they can be chemically guaranteed to cause them – artificially elevating or depressing neurotransmitter levels in a way that may affect not only mood, but all the body's most basic regulatory systems.

The principal 'evidence' for the therapeutic efficacy of psychopharmaceutical medications comes from short-term clinically controlled studies comparing the effects of an active drug with that of an inactive or 'inert' placebo. In most cases, the difference between the drug and placebo thought necessary to scientifically 'prove' the efficacy of the former is minimal. But comparing the effects of any active drug with an inert placebo is, as Breggin points out, misleading in itself. This is because the active drug may have its own type of placebo effect – giving the patient a felt sense of a drug's power by virtue of its felt effects, however subtle.

As Grohol points out:

"the double-blind placebo controlled study is not blind. Side effects are so obvious that more than 80% of the patients know whether they are on active medication or placebo, patients are equally accurate about other patients on the ward, and nurses and other personnel are privy as well. In some studies the only people who claim to be blind are the prescribing physicians, and in other studies the prescribing physicians admit being as aware of the patients' condition as everyone else." Even with active placebos "the empirical data show that medication effect sizes are hard to distinguish from the placebo. Also not mentioned is that most antidepressant medications habituate, and the patients' symptoms return. Most patients believe they would feel even worse if they were not taking their medication."

Grohol goes on to question the use of clinician-rated rather than patient-rated measures of 'improvement' in such trials, noting that "If patients cannot tell that they are better off in a controlled study, one must question the conventional wisdom about the efficacy of antidepressant drugs."

One of the main arguments in favour of the use of anti-depressants is suicide and violence prevention. How is it then, that several studies have shown an actual increase in suicide rates in those taking anti-depressants? How is that otherwise sober and responsible individuals with no history of violence or severe personality disorder can, within a few day or weeks fall victim to violent or suicidal impulses, even to the point of committing murder or suicide? One reason is the stimulant effect of the new Prozac-type antidepressants or Selective Serotonin Reuptake Inhibitors (SSRIs). The artificially elevated serotonin levels they are designed to induce can result not only in mild euphoria but manic states or psychotic syndromes similar to those produced by illegal amphetamines. Alternatively, they may, in the first few days of usage result in an unnatural depression of serotonin levels as the brain tries to compensate for an artificially induced chemical imbalance. In both cases the drug has brought about a form of organic brain dysfunction of the very sort assumed, without evidence, to be responsible for the patient's symptoms. Another argument for the use of anti-depressants is their 'efficacy' for many people. No thought is given however, as to the reasons why such drugs are felt or deemed to be 'effective'. Breggin points out that "A patient typically is rendered unable to stay depressed during an episode of organic brain dysfunction, because depression requires a relatively intact brain and mind. Rendered either apathetic or artificially euphoric by brain dysfunction, the patient is evaluated as 'improved'."

"What psychiatrists call 'depression' – lethargy, apathy, nervousness, hopelessness, helplessness and unhappiness – is a serious problem often unrecognised as drug-related. Because of their depressant and debilitating effect, psychiatric drugs can make people feel so bad they want to kill themselves."

Caligari

SSRI's such as paroxetine (Seroxat/Paxil) and Prozac may be authorised for use by patients over many years on the basis of clinical trials lasting from only 6 to 10 weeks. GlaxoSmithKline, whose sales of Seroxat/Paxil were valued at over one and a half billion pounds in 2000, continue aggressive marketing of the drug to doctors, with 100 millions prescriptions given annually. This despite the fact that their own staff reported trial patients showing significant withdrawal symptoms of agitation and insomnia after only a short period on the drug – which now leads the list the World Health Organisation list of pharmaceuticals reported by doctors to cause acute withdrawal problems. A GSK leaflet accompanying prescriptions still tells the patient that "you cannot become addicted to Seroxat." No distinction is made between dependency of the sort comparable to an addicts cravings for tobacco or heroin, and addiction based purely on the need to avoid acute physical or psychological withdrawal symptoms. The information leaflet for Seroxat also includes the following words:

"Occasionally, the symptoms of depression may include thoughts of harming yourself or committing suicide. Until the full antidepressant effect of your medication becomes apparent it is possible that these symptoms may increase in the first few weeks of treatment."

The tone is soothing. But in June 2001, GSK were forced to pay out $6.4 million in damages to the family of a man who killed his wife, daughter, granddaughter and then himself after only two days on Seroxat.

In contrast to the SSRIs, most *neuroleptic* drugs or 'anti-psychotics', together with the minor and major tranquillizers, work by dulling and depressing brain activity through a wide range of different neurotransmitters including dopamine and GABA. The artificially-induced elevation or depression of mood brought on by the elevation or depression of different neurotransmitters in the brain, may have dramatic effects when the drug is *withdrawn* – either producing a dramatic 'rebound' elevation of neurotransmitter levels or leaving the brain incapable of generating normal neurotransmitter levels by itself. Breggin cites a typical example of withdrawal syndrome:

"Recently one of my patients, a young man in his twenties, was trying to taper off small doses of Elavil prescribed by another physician…within a day or two of complete withdrawal he began to feel ill. It seemed exactly like the flu. He felt lethargic and his muscles ached, he lacked appetite, felt sick to his stomach, and vomited in the morning. Despite his tiredness he had trouble falling asleep and staying asleep. He felt increasing anxiety as well. A complete physical examination by an internist revealed no evidence of an infection, and I was forced to conclude that he had a typical flu-like withdrawal syndrome. He gradually recovered over a few weeks, vomiting for the last time about a month after ending the medication."

Not all are as 'lucky' as this patient. Countless harrowing stories by those who became unknowingly dependent on highly-addictive *benzodiazepine* tranquillizers and sleeping pills, or so-called 'non-addictive' anti-depressants, bear testament to the years or even decades of hell suffered in the attempt to withdraw from these drugs, and/or of the permanent post-withdrawal symptoms they still suffer. With one out of four people in the UK thought to be suffering from a diagnosable mental disorder, the number of prescriptions of anti-depressants and anxiolytics is vast. As long ago as 1984, it was reported by Professor Malcom Lader that 11.2 percent of all adults took a *benzodiazepine* for anxiety or sleeping problems in any one year. "Even at a conservative estimate, 20% of these will develop symptoms when they attempt to withdraw. That means a quarter of a million people in the UK. It is now estimated that one and a half million people in the UK alone are chronically addicted to one of the many benzodiazepine 'anxiolytics' such as diazepam (Valium) and lorazepam (Ativan). All the drugs in this class can induce dependency in a matter of days through suppressing the brain's natural production of anxiety- and stress-reducing neurotransmitters. Yet they account for 50% of global sales of psychopharmaceutical medications.

"The biggest drug-addiction problem in the world doesn't involve heroin, cocaine or marijuana. In fact, it doesn't involve an illegal drug at all. The world's biggest drug-addiction problem is posed by a group of drugs, the *benzodiazepines*, which are widely prescribed by doctors and taken by countless millions of perfectly ordinary people around the world... Drug-addiction experts claim that getting people off the benzodiazepines is more difficult than getting addicts off heroin... For several years now pressure-groups have been fighting to help addicted individuals break free from their pharmacological chains. But the fight has been a forlorn one. As fast as one individual breaks free from one of the benzodiazepines another patient somewhere else becomes addicted. I believe that the main reason for this is that doctors are addicted to prescribing benzodiazepines just as much as patients are hooked on taking them."

Vernon Coleman, *Life Without Tranquillizers*

The sheer scale of the problem with psychopharmaceutical medications becomes clear if we consider that probably 75% or more of so-called 'adverse reactions', including withdrawal symptoms and withdrawal syndromes, may be unreported. Worse still, they may be unrecognised as such by patients themselves, interpreted as signs of endogenous psychological disorders by physicians or psychotherapists, and/or treated by prescriptions of further psychiatric drugs. In an attempt to deal with recognised side-effects of these drugs, many psychiatrists and psychiatric health clinics around the world now regularly prescribe whole 'cocktails' of anti-depressant, neuroleptic and anxiolytic medications in the hope that they will chemically counter-balance each other's inherently toxic and unbalancing effects on brain functioning. At the same time pharmaceutical companies such as GSK are inventing ever new 'disorders' which can be 'treated' by drugs such as paroxetine. As well as 'panic disorder', 'obsessive compulsive disorder' the list now includes 'post-traumatic stress disorder' and 'social anxiety disorder' and 'attention deficit disorder'. But like standard DSM psychiatric designations such as 'bipolar disorder', 'personality disorder', these new terms for new 'disorders' seem to possess the authority of medical diagnoses – implying the existence of specific disease entities with an organic basis. In fact they are merely convenient labels for clusters of troublesome symptoms or behaviours that society has a problem understanding and responding to.

Biological psychiatry is founded on a flat denial that there is any meaning in 'mental illness' – that in a sick society there may be good reasons why a person feels anxious, depressed, disturbed, divided or driven to compulsive behaviours. Health is defined only as the ability to 'function' normally as an employee – to cheerfully play one's part in sustaining a market economy in which all human relations are geared solely to commodity production and profit making. As a result, medicine and psychiatry have both become tools of the 'therapeutic state' – their sole aim being to control all bodily behavioural symptoms of the distress and dis-ease engendered by a sick society, reducing them instead to some manageable disease or psychiatric disorder that can be 'managed' with the help of drugs – thereby turning them into a lucrative source of corporate profit.

Authoritarian psychiatry is now being legitimised by governments all over the world through legislation which denies mental patients the right to refuse medication and permits their enforced detention and drug 'treatment'. Given the enormous attention given by politicians and the media to the problems caused by illegal drugs and drug addiction, the failure by governments and health services to recognise the scale of addiction to legally prescribed drugs and the dangers of their adverse effects is hypocritical to say the least – amounting to a form of wilful ignorance. It is all the more important then, that social workers, mental health nurses, counsellors, psychotherapists and alternative health practitioners do not fall into the trap that so many orthodox physicians and psychiatrists have fallen into – that of accepting the medical and marketing myths perpetuated by pharmaceutical companies regarding the 'benefits' of psychiatric medications. Above all it is important that they:

1. obtain precise details of any client's present or past use, not only of illegal drugs but of legally prescribed medications, including the names of these medications and the length of time over which they were or have been taken.

2. educate themselves in the adverse effects, addictive potentials and withdrawal symptoms of specific anxiolytic, anti-depressant and neuroleptic medications.

Thankfully, the internet now offers access to detailed information regarding prescription drugs, as well as being host to sites set up to support patients suffering from adverse reactions or dependency, to inform of their dangers, to advise on safe methods of withdrawal, or to provide blogs and forums in which users can share their often horrifying experiences of particular medications and their debilitating or life-destroying effects.

Recommended sites:

www.benzo.org.uk info. – on benzodiazepines
www.antidepressantfacts.com
www.Breggin.com excellent articles by Peter Breggin
www.pssg.org for Prozac survivors
www.antipsychiatry.org the case against biopsychiatry
www.april.org.uk on adverse drug reactions)
www.mindfreedom.org supporting patients

Recommended Reading:

Peter R. Breggin *Toxic Psychiatry*
Breggin/Cohen *Your Drug May be Your Problem*
Joan E. Gadsby *Addiction by Prescription*
Heather Jones *Prisoner on Prescription*
David Smail *The Nature of Unhappiness*
Dr Ann Tracy *Prozac – Panacea or Pandora*
Robert Whitaker *Anatomy of an Epidemic: Magic Bullets, Psychiatric Drugs, and the Astonishing Rise of Mental Illness in America*

Research sources:

Fisher, S., & Greenberg, R.P. (1993). *How sound is the double-blind design for evaluating psychotropic drugs?* The Journal of Nervous and Mental Disease, 181, 345-350.

Greenberg, R.P., Bornstein, R.F., Greenberg, M.D., & Fisher, S. (1992). *A meta-analysis of antidepressant outcome under "blinder" conditions.* Journal of Consulting and Clinical Psychology, 60, 664-66

Jay C. Fournier, MA; Robert J. DeRubeis, PhD; Steven D. Hollon, PhD; Sona Dimidjian, PhD; Jay D. Amsterdam, MD; Richard C. Shelton, MD; Jan Fawcett, MD *Antidepressant Drug Effects and Depression Severity – A Patient-Level Meta-analysis* Journal of the American Medical Association. 2010;303(1)

Harrow M, Jobe TH *Factors involved in outcome and recovery in schizophrenia patients not on antipsychotic medications: a 15-year multifollow-up study.* Department of Psychiatry, University of Illinois College of Medicine, Chicago, Illinois, USA. mharrow@psych.uic.edu

'The Awareness Principle' summarised

Definition

A new philosophical foundation for counselling and psychotherapy, medicine and psychiatry, science and life.

Roots

The 'A-dvaita' or 'non-dual' school of Indian philosophy. In particular the schools of yoga and philosophical theology known collectively as 'Shaiva Advaita', 'Shaivist Tantrism' or 'Kashmir Shaivism'.

Basic Principle

Awareness as such and anything we are or could be aware of are like two sides of a coin, both inseparable and perfectly distinct.

Similarly the whole principle of 'monism', 'unity' or 'non-duality' implies neither separation nor loss of all distinction.

The true 'monistic' principle of 'non-duality' is inseparable distinction.

Space and Awareness 1

We are aware of things in space.

Those things cannot be separated from the empty space around or within them (atoms are largely space too).

Nevertheless that space remains absolutely distinct from anything and everything we are aware of in it.

Like 'empty' space, awareness as such – 'pure' awareness' – cannot be separated from particular, tangible things we are aware of.

Nevertheless it remains absolutely distinct from them.

Space and Awareness 2

If there were no such thing as space itself we could not be aware of anything within it. Space as such is therefore the pre-condition for us being aware of anything in it.

Similarly, awareness as such is the precondition for us being aware of anything at all, including space itself.

Ultimately, what we perceive as 'empty' space is nothing but the field of pure awareness necessary for us to be aware or 'conscious' of anything at all within it.

Space is essentially nothing 'physical' or 'objective'. Instead it is a dimension of awareness or subjectivity – one way of experiencing pure awareness.

'Awareness' and 'Consciousness' 1

Awareness and 'consciousness' are inseparable and yet fundamentally distinct.

If people 'lose themselves' through absorption in watching TV or a movie, reading a book or playing computer games, in work or domestic chores, in talking or making love, in sensations of pleasure or pain, or just in trains of thought or strong emotions, then they are still 'conscious' – but they are not fully aware.

'Awareness' and 'Consciousness' 2

Whenever our 'consciousness' becomes overly focussed on, fixated by, absorbed in or identified with any one thing, we lose awareness of our body and sensory environment as a whole, and all the other things and bodies within it.

In this sense, 'consciousness' is contracted awareness.

If, on the other hand, we can experience something or engage in some activity without losing a more expanded consciousness – one that can simultaneously embrace other things, thoughts, feelings and possible activities within it – then we are aware.

In this sense 'awareness' is expanded consciousness.

Awareness, Consciousness and Space

Awareness has the same nature as space. It always embraces countless things, and can never be fully absorbed in, or contained by or reduced to any one thing or set of things.

Like time, space is a dimension of awareness – understood as an expanded and ultimately unbounded spacious field of consciousness.

In this sense awareness is *field consciousness*.

Consciousness on the other hand, is the contraction of this field of awareness to a specific focus.

In this sense consciousness is *focal awareness*.

Locality and Non-Locality

We can locate an object 'in' space, but space as such, even though it can be divided and has many dimensions, has no location.

Similarly, awareness has an essentially non-local or field character.

Awareness fields are essentially non-local, whereas anything we are conscious of or aware of within them has a local or localisable character – whether an object in space, a feeling we experience in a part of our body, or a thought we are aware of in our head.

Loci and Foci of Awareness

Awareness is ultimately one singular, multidimensional field.

Every thing and every being in that field is a specific centre or 'locus' of awareness.

It is also a possible 'focus' of awareness for another such locus of awareness.

Each of us is a centre or locus of awareness able to focus our awareness on other such centres or loci of awareness – whether in the form of things or people.

As centres or loci of awareness, each of us is also but one centre or locus of a singular, multi-dimensional awareness field.

The One and the Many

The infinite, multidimensional awareness field is 'God' – the source of everything and every being.

Every thing and being is a unique field-pattern of awareness, one that in turn shapes its own uniquely patterned awareness field – its own uniquely perceived experiential world or environment.

The divine awareness field is therefore a field of fields – a holofield embracing the individual awareness fields of every thing and being.

We perceive all things according to our own field-patterns of awareness and from our own centres or loci of awareness.

Yet what we perceive is itself a unique field-pattern of awareness with its own uniquely patterned awareness field or experiential world.

Unity in Diversity

What unites all things and beings is that they are each centres of the infinite multi-dimensional world of awareness that is God, and that their own individual experienced worlds or awareness fields are but one part of that larger and divine 'field of fields' or 'Holofield'.

Each individual's awareness field is bounded only by the limitations and horizon of their own awareness.

The divine awareness field is unbounded and yet it both embraces and experiences itself through the individual awareness fields of each and every being, knowing itself as their common source and centre.

This common source and centre is God – understood as a divine "singularity of awareness" (Michael Kosok) uniting all individual centres of awareness as their essential or divine 'Self', and uniting also all the individual awareness fields that make up their experiential and perceptual Worlds.

Personalised Training in ABCT

Training in ABCT is intended primarily for counsellors, psychotherapists, psychologists, and other health, educational or social work professionals seeking an alternative to conventional CBT trainings – and/or wishing to integrate 'education in awareness' into their existing professional work.

Its principle aim is to cultivate the individual's capacity to articulate, apply, teach and *live* the basic principle and practices of awareness on which ABCT is founded – and to embody them in both their professional and personal life and relationships.

Since counselling and psychotherapy, as well as many others forms of personalised education, health care and social work, are conducted principally in a one-to-one setting or on a one-to-one basis, so also is training in ABCT, which takes the form of regular half-day personal training sessions – arranged at intervals suited to each trainee and geared both to their personal background, skills and purposes and to the pace of their progress in training.

This Personalised Training in ABCT not only offers great flexibility to the potential trainee, but also allows for a *seamless and continuous path of learning* leading from personal therapy and 'education in awareness' to supervised professional practice and integrating both under the attuned and aware guidance of the same mentor.

The only prerequisites for trainees in ABCT are a suitable degree of competence in basic study, writing, listening, speaking and teaching skills, and a basic commitment to the continuous and diligent practice of meditative awareness in the context of both their personal and professional life.

For more information e-mail or write to 'Education in Awareness', including both CV and a minimum one-page biography – including a description of any other forms of meditation or therapy that you have studied, undergone, practiced, written about or taught.

Contact details:

Karin Heinitz
Education in Awareness (ABCT)
Cromwell Rd. Counselling and Meditation Centre
Whitstable, Kent
CT5 1NF

e-mail: abct@cromwellroadcentre.co.uk

Peter Wilberg (BA Oxon, MA Humanistic Psychology) is an independent non-institutional thinker in the radical tradition of Ivan Illich. In addition to his wide range of books, he has contributed articles on psychotherapy to both the Journal of Biosynthesis and the Journal of the Society for Existential Analysis. Born in London in 1952, he lives in Whitstable, U.K.

Other Books by Peter Wilberg:

The Awareness Principle – a radical new philosophy of life, science and religion
New Yoga Publications 2009

Tantric Wisdom for Today's World –The New Yoga of Awareness
New Yoga Publications 2009

Tantra Reborn – the sensuality and sexuality of your immortal soul body
New Yoga Publications 2009

Heidegger, Phenomenology and Indian Thought
New Yoga Publications 2008

What is Hinduism? – radical new perspectives on the most ancient of religions
New Yoga Publications 2009

Event Horizon – terror, tantra and the ultimate metaphysics of awareness
New Yoga Publications 2008

The Science Delusion – why God is real and science is religious myth
New Yoga Publications 2008

Heidegger, Medicine and 'Scientific Method' – the unheeded heritage of the Zollikon Seminars New Gnosis Publications 2005

The Therapist as Listener – Heidegger and the missing dimension of counselling and psychotherapy training New Gnosis Publications 2005

The QUALIA Revolution – from quantum physics to qualia science
Second Edition New Gnosis Publications 2008

From New Age to New Gnosis – towards a new gnostic spirituality
New Gnosis Publications 2003

Head, Heart and Hara – the soul centres of West and East
New Gnosis Publications, 2003

Deep Socialism – a new manifesto of Marxist ethics and economics
New Gnosis Publications 2003

LaVergne, TN USA
23 February 2011
217647LV00003B/68/P